Bicycle Trails

of

Illinois

4th Edition

An American Bike Trails Publication

Bicycle Trails
of Illinois

4th Edition

Published by   American Bike Trails

Created by   Ray Hoven

Design by   Mary C. Rumpsa

Table of Contents

Table of Contents (continued)

Additional Trails

Indices

How To Use This Book

This book provides a comprehensive, easy-to-use quick reference to most of the off-road trails throughout Illinois. It contains over 120 detailed trail maps, plus overviews covering the state sectionally, selective counties and city areas. Detail trail maps are listed alphabetically. The sectional overviews are grouped near the front, with a section cross-referencing counties and towns to trails, and a section listing many of the parks in Illinois with their pertinent information. Each trail map includes such helpful features as location and access, trail facilities, nearby communities and their populations.

Terms Used

Length Expressed in miles. Round trip mileage is normally indicated for loops.

Effort Levels *Easy* Physical exertion is not strenuous. Climbs and descents as well as technical obstacles are more minimal. Recommended for beginners.

      Moderate Physical exertion is not excessive. Climbs and descents can be challenging. Expect some technical obstacles.

      Difficult Physical exertion is demanding. Climbs and descents require good riding skills. Trail surface may be sandy, loose rock, soft or wet.

Directions Describes by way of directions and distances, how to get to the trail areas from roads and nearby communities.

Map Illustrative representation of a geographic area, such as a state, section, forest, park or trail complex.

Forest Typically encompasses a dense growth of trees and underbrush covering a large tract.

Park A tract of land generally including woodlands and open areas.

DNR Department of Natural Resources

Types of Biking

Mountain Fat-tired bikes are recommended. Ride may be generally flat but then with a soft, rocky or wet surface.

Leisure Off-road gentle ride. Surface is generally paved or screened.

Tour Riding on roads with motorized traffic or on road shoulders.

Riding Tips

Pushing in gears that are too high can push knees beyond their limits. Avoid extremes by pedaling faster rather than shifting into a higher gear.

Keeping your elbows bent, changing your hand position frequently and wearing bicycle gloves all help to reduce the numbness or pain in the palm of the hand from long-distance riding.

Keep you pedal rpms up on an uphill so you have reserve power if you lose speed.

Stay in a high-gear on a level surface, placing pressure on the pedals and resting on the handle bars and saddle.

Lower your center of gravity on a long or steep downhill run by using the quick release seat post binder and dropping the saddle height down.

Brake intermittently on a rough surface.

Wear proper equipment. Wear a helmet that is approved by the Snell Memorial Foundation or the American National Standards Institute. Look for one of their stickers inside the helmet.

Use a lower tire inflation pressure for riding on unpaved surfaces. The lower pressure will provide better tire traction and a more comfortable ride.

Apply your brakes gradually to maintain control on loose gravel or soil.

Ride only on trails designated for bicycles or in areas where you have the permission of the landowner.

Be courteous to hikers or horseback riders on the trail, they have the right of way.

Leave riding trails in the condition you found them. Be sensitive to the environment. Properly dispose of your trash. If you open a gate, close it behind you.

Don't carry items or attach anything to your bicycle that might hinder your vision or control.

Don't wear anything that restricts your hearing.

Don't carry extra clothing where it can hang down and jam in a wheel.

Explanation of Symbols

TRAIL USES

 Mountain Biking

 Leisure Biking

 In Line Skating

 Cross-Country Skiing

 Hiking

 Horseback Riding

Snowmobiling

ROUTES

━━━━━ Multi-Use Trail

▪▪▪▪▪▪▪ Bikeway Trail

•••••• Equestrian Trail

▪▪▪▪▪▪▪ Alternate Bike Trail

▪ ▪ ▪ ▪ ▪ ▪ Alternate Trail

===== Planned Trail

╬╬╬╬╬╬╬ Railroad Tracks

━━━━ Roadway

FACILITIES

 Bike Repair

 Camping

 First Aid

 Info

 Lodging

 Parking

 Picnic

 Refreshments

 Restrooms

 Shelter

 Water

 Multi Facilities Available

Refreshments	First Aid
Telephone	Picnic
Restrooms	Lodging

ROAD RELATED SYMBOLS

 Interstate Highway

12 U.S. Highway

26 State Highway

K County Highway

AREA DESCRIPTIONS

City, Town

Parks, Preserves

Waterway

▪━▪━ Mileage Scale

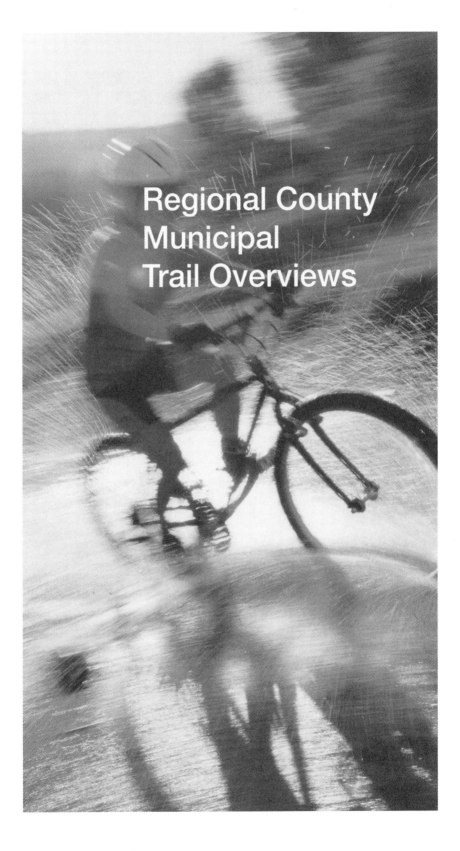

Regional County Municipal Trail Overviews

State of Illinois

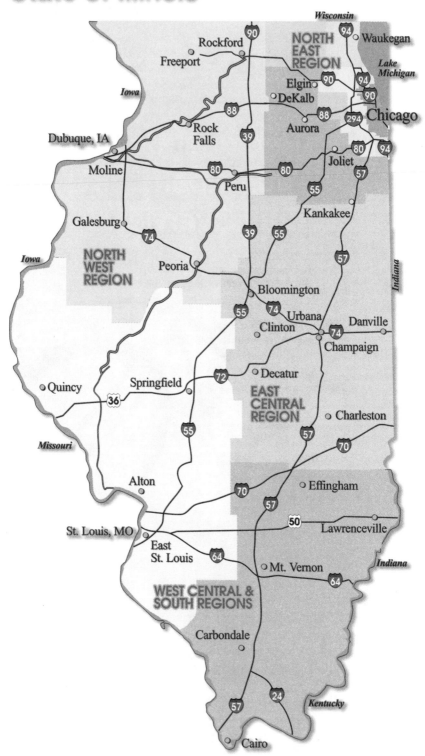

Mileage Between Principal Cities

CITY	SPRINGFIELD	ST. LOUIS, MO	ROCKFORD	PEORIA	CHICAGO	CHAMPAIGN
BLOOMINGTON	64	163	136	40	136	53
CAIRO	242	148	426	312	375	244
CARBONDALE	172	108	384	242	333	202
CHAMPAIGN	86	182	188	92	137	
CHICAGO	201	300	83	170		137
DECATUR	39	118	179	83	178	47
DE KALB	183	282	44	124	66	174
DUBUQUE, IA	238	337	91	167	176	259
EFFINGHAM	89	104	260	164	209	78
ELGIN	208	307	48	148	37	169
GALESBURG	120	219	150	49	198	141
KANKAKEE	158	254	138	121	56	78
LAWRENCEVILLE	154	147	309	213	250	127
MOLINE	163	262	117	92	165	184
MT. VERNON	146	82	330	216	279	148
PEORIA	71	170	138		170	92
QUINCY	110	133	269	131	310	195
ROCKFORD	197	296		138	83	188
ST. LOUIS, MO	100		296	170	300	182
SPRINGFIELD		100	197	71	201	86
WAUKEGAN	229	328	71	198	40	181

North West Region

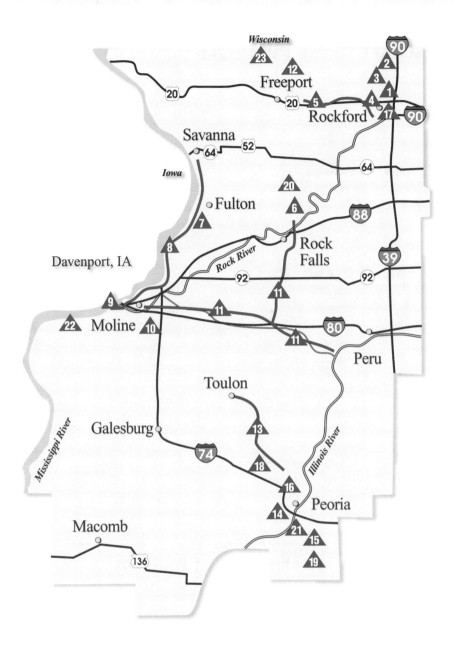

Wisconsin

Freeport

Rockford

Savanna

Iowa

Fulton

Davenport, IA

Rock Falls

Moline

Peru

Toulon

Galesburg

Peoria

Macomb

Mississippi River

Rock River

Illinois River

20

20

5

23

12

2

3

4

1

17

90

90

64

52

20

6

88

39

7

8

92

92

9

11

22

10

11

11

80

13

74

18

16

14

21

15

19

136

13

North East Region

Planning for that Trail Visit

Checkoff List

Information you may want to have at hand

- ☐ Trail location
- ☐ Trail accesses
- ☐ Parking
- ☐ Restrooms
- ☐ Drinking water
- ☐ Refreshments
- ☐ Lodging
- ☐ Conditions
- ☐ Local area events
- ☐ Telephone access
- ☐ Bicycle service
- ☐ Picnic facilities
- ☐ Shelters
- ☐ Camping facilities
- ☐ Emergency assistance phone number

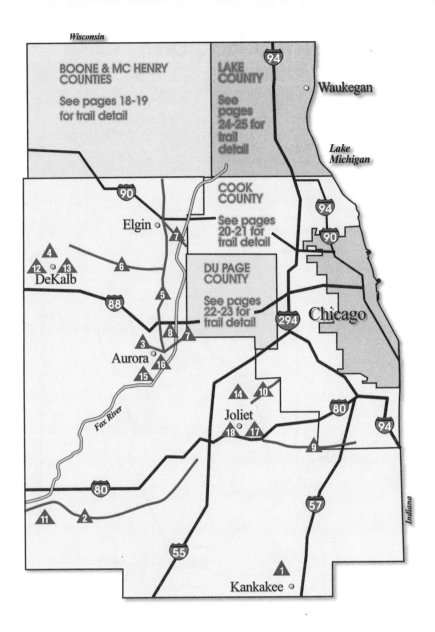

Comprehensive bikeway maps of the Chicago
metropolitan area are available for $7.00 plus $1.90
postage from:

Bikeways
Northeastern Illinois Planning Commission
400 W. Madison Street, Room 200
Chicago, IL 60606

East Central Region

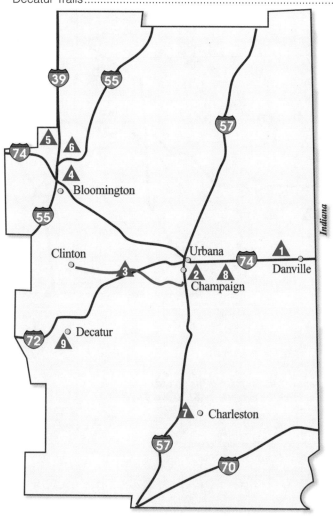

West Central & South Regions

Boone and McHenry Counties

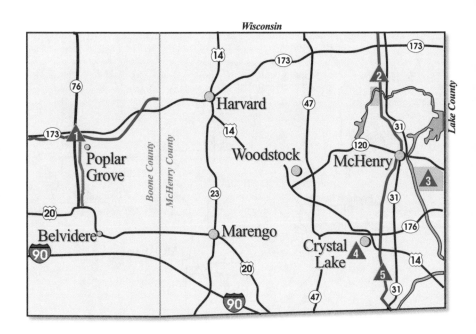

Crystal Lake Trails

	Prairie Trail	Sterne's Woods	Veteran Acres	W. Herrick Lippold Pk.	Winding Creek
Trail Length	18 mi.	2.1 mi.	7.5 mi.	3.5 mi.	2.5 mi.
Surface	pvd./scrn'g	paved/dirt road	paved/natural	screenings	paved
Uses*	L, H	F, H, X	F, H, X	L, H	L, S

Location & Setting These trails are located throughout the Crystal Lake area. McHenry County is a favorite destination for water sport activities by Chicagoland residents.

Information Crystal Lake Park District   (815) 459-0680
One East Crystal Lake Avenue
Crystal Lake, IL 60014

County McHenry

●*See Detail Maps*

---

* USES
L = Leisure Bicycling   F = Fat Tire Bicycling   H = Hiking, Jogging   L
                    S = in-line skating   X = Cross country skiing

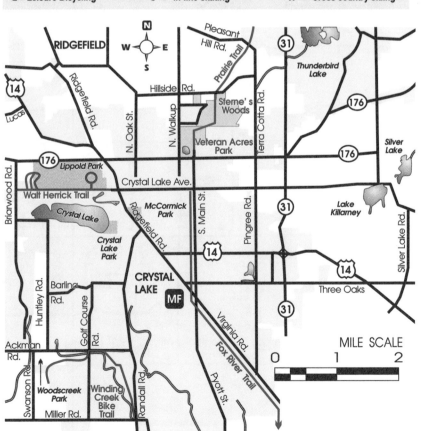

Champaign County

Trail Length	Approximately 18 miles of bike path (plus over 30 miles of bike routes)
Surface	Paved
Location & Setting	The cities of Champaign and Urbana in east central Illinois. The paths generally parallel streets or through parks. The setting is urban and is the home of the University of Illinois.
Information	Champaign County Regional Planning Commission (217) 328-3313
County	Champaign

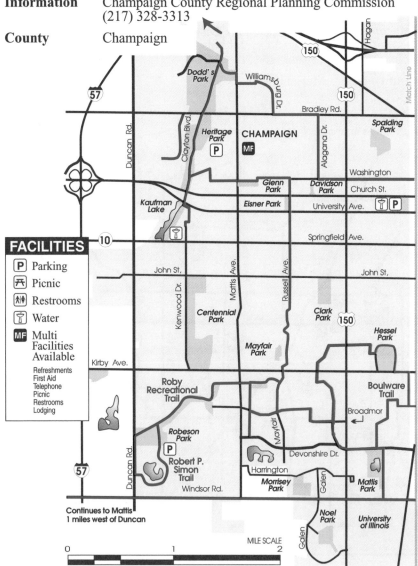

FACILITIES

- P Parking
- ⛱ Picnic
- 🚻 Restrooms
- 🚰 Water
- MF Multi Facilities Available

Refreshments
First Aid
Telephone
Picnic
Restrooms
Lodging

MILE SCALE

0   1   2

ROUTES

Bicycling Trail
Bikeway
Roadway

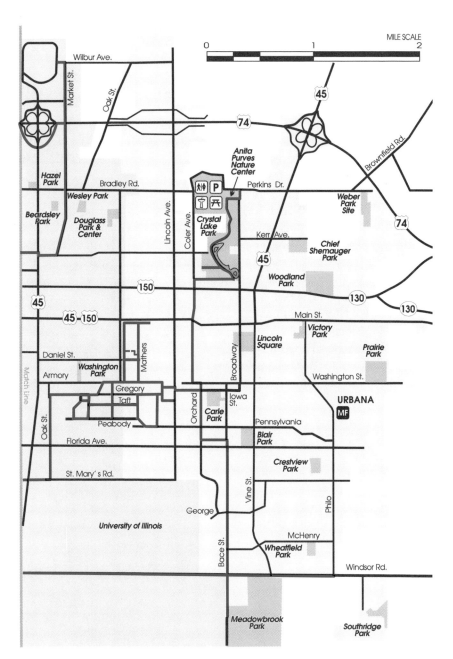

MILE SCALE

Wilbur Ave.

Market St.

Oak St.

74

45

Brownfield Rd.

Hazel Park

Bradley Rd.

Anita Purves Nature Center

Perkins Dr.

Weber Park Site

Wesley Park

Lincoln Ave.

Coler Ave.

Crystal Lake Park

Kerr Ave.

74

Beardsley Park

Douglass Park & Center

45

Chief Shemauger Park

Woodland Park

150

45

45–150

130

130

Main St.

Daniel St.

Mathers

Victory Park

Prairie Park

Washington Park

Broadway

Lincoln Square

Washington St.

Armory

Gregory

Taft

Orchard

Iowa St.

URBANA
MF

Match Line

Oak St.

Peabody

Carle Park

Pennsylvania

Florida Ave.

Blair Park

St. Mary's Rd.

Crestview Park

Vine St.

George

University of Illinois

Race St.

Philo

McHenry

Wheatfield Park

Windsor Rd.

Meadowbrook Park

Southridge Park

Cook County

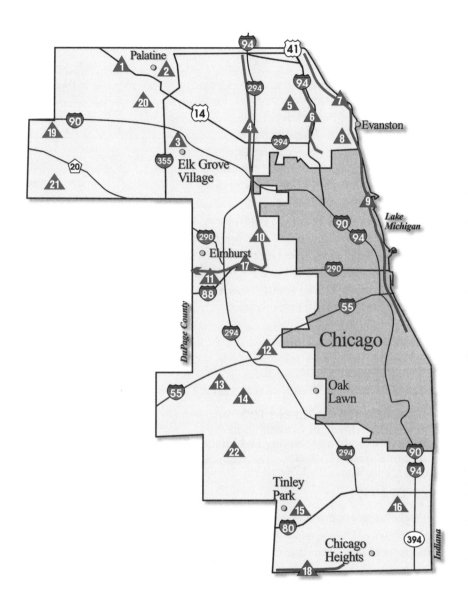

Palatine

1
2
20
14
294
94
7
90
19
5
6
Evanston
20
4
294
8
355
3
Elk Grove
Village
9
90
94
Lake
Michigan
290
10
Elmhurst
290
17
11
88
55
DuPage County
294
Chicago
12
55
13
14
Oak
Lawn
22
294
90
94
Tinley
Park
15
16
80
Chicago
Heights
394
Indiana
18

DuPage County

Bicycle Resources

Bicycling (Brochure) Free

Illinois Department of Conservation
Office of Resource Marketing and Education
524 South Second Street
Springfield, IL 62701-1787

(217)782-7454

Information brochure listing off-road bicycle trails statewide. The Department of Conservation also distributes an attractive Illinois State Parks magazine as well as brochures on hiking, camping, and other outdoor activities.

Illinois Visitor's Guide

Illinois Dept. of Commerce and Community Affairs
Bureau of Tourism
620 East Adams Street
Springfield, IL 62701

(800)223-0121

Lists campgrounds, hotels and motels, and recreational and cultural attractions throughout the state.

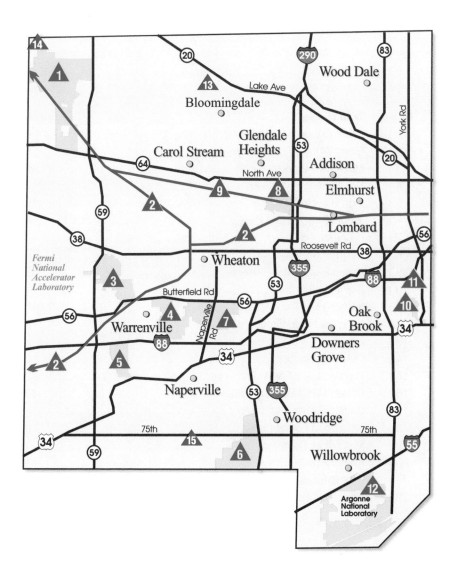

Lake County

Bicycle Maintenance Checklist
Inspect your bicycle for the following:

Tires should not have cracks on the sidewalls, cuts in the tread or excessive wear. Using proper tire pressure, printed on the sidewall of the tire, prevents excessive wear.

Gear and brake cables move freely. Replace rusted or frayed cables.

The chain should be free of rust. Too much oil will attract dust and dirt, shortening the life of the chain.

Pedals are securely fastened, and pedal reflectors are clean and visible.

This checklist takes only a few minutes and may prevent you from having an accident or mechanical breakdown.

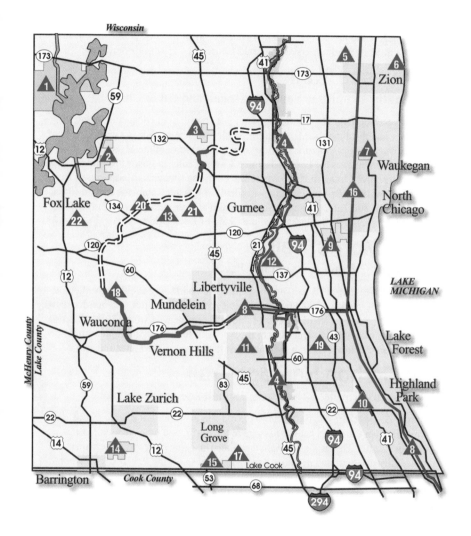

Wisconsin

Zion

Waukegan

North
Chicago

Fox Lake

Gurnee

LAKE
MICHIGAN

Libertyville

Mundelein

Wauconda

Vernon Hills

Lake
Forest

Lake Zurich

Highland
Park

Long
Grove

Lake Cook

Barrington   Cook County

McHenry County

Lake County

Madison County Trails

Bluff Trail

Trail Length 2 miles   **Surface** Paved

Location & Setting A 2 mile, asphalt trail connecting the Nature
Trail at the Southern Illinois University campus to the south and the on-road bikeway
on New Poag Road to the north. Parking is available on Bluff Road at the SIUE Delyte
Morris trail, at Korte Stadium and at St. Paul's Church of Christ in Edwardsville.

Confluence Trail

Trail Length 16 miles   **Surface** Asphalt and Oil & Chip

Location & Setting The Confluence Trail is a 16 mile trail connecting Alton to
Granite City, mainly along the Mississippi River levee. The surface is a combination of
asphalt and oil and chip. The ride provides spectacular views of the Mississippi River,
and popular stops such as the Lock & Dam 26 Visitor Center in East Alton and the Lewis
& Clark Interpretive Center in Hartford. It also connects Illinois to Missouri over the
historic Chain of Rock Bridge. Parking is available at Russell Commons Park in Alton,
the Lock & Dam 26 Visitor Center, the Lewis & Clark Interpretive Center in Hartford,
and both the Illinois and Missouri side of the Chain of Rock Bridge.

Delyte Morris Trail

Trail Length 2.8 miles   **Surface** Paved

Location & Setting This path proceeds from the courthouse in Edwardsville to Bluff
Road on the western edge of the Southern Illinois University campus. From Edwardsville
the trail continues down a small valley and through some heavily wooded area. Sections
are rugged with hilly terrain. Once out of the woods, it follows an old railroad right-of-
way through prairie areas. Parking is available at the Cougar Lake recreation area.

Glen Carbon Heritage Trail

Trail Length 11 miles   **Surface** Asphalt and crushed stone

Location & Setting The trail follows the old Illinois Central RR route from Hwy
255, through Glen Carbon, a natural passage in the bluffs, and onto restored prairies
on top of the bluffs. The surface is asphalt and merimac gravel. Parking, restroom and
picnic facilities can be found in Miner Park, a few blocks off the trail in Glen Carbon.
Along the trail are several historical markers and 8 timber trestle bridges. The Silver
Creek Railroad trestle is 340 feet long. Glen Carbon is located in Madison County by the
confluence of Hwy 70, 55, 270 and 255. A good trail starting off point is from behind the
fire station in Glen Carbon or from Miner Park.

Nature Trail

Trail Length 12 miles   **Surface** Asphalt

Location & Setting The Nature Trail is built along the old Illinois Terminal Railroad
line. It begins at Hwy 159 and Longfellow Rd in Edwardsville near the Lewis & Clark
Community College N.O. Nelson campus, continuing through the Southern Illinois
University Edwardsville campus, and then southwest to Lake Dr in Pontoon Beach.
Parking is available at the St. Paul United Church of Christ at Longfellow Rd and Nelson
Ave, at Longfellow Rd at Hwy 159 in Edwardsville, and at Revelle Ln in Pontoon Beach.

Nickel Plate Trail

Trail Length 4.6 miles **Surface** Crushed limestone

Location & Setting The 4.6 mile Nickel Plate Trail is built along a section of the New York, Toledo, St. Louis Railroad line nicknamed the "Nickel Plate." It connects the Nature Trail to the west edge of the Glen Carbon Heritage Trail. The surface is crushed limestone. It begins at Hwy 159 and Longfellow Road in Edwardsville and extends south to the Glen Carbon Heritage Trail at Main Street in Glen Carbon.

Parking is available at Longfellow Road at Nelson Avenue, at Longfellow Road at Hwy 159 adjacent to the LCCC N.O. Nelson campus in Edwardsville, and at Main Street in Glen Carbon behind the ball field.

Quercus Grove Trail

Trail Length 3 miles **Surface** Asphalt

Location & Setting The Quercus Grove Trail is a 3-mile asphalt trail beginning at the Nickel Plate Trail, at the intersection of Schwarz and Springer Streets in downtown Edwardsville, and extending northeast along Hwy 157 to Hazel Road in rural Edwardsville where it ends.

Parking is available in Edwardsville at the Park and Ride Lot for the Madison County Transit Edwardsville Station.

Schoolhouse Trail

Trail Length 11.5 miles **Surface** Asphalt

Location & Setting The Schoolhouse Trail connects the communities of Collinsville, Maryville, Troy, Granite City and Pontoon Beach. The surface is asphalt. The trail begins at the intersection of Hwy 162 and Edwardsville/Troy Road in Troy and extends past Drost Park in Maryville to Horseshoe Lake State Park in Granite City. There is an on-road bikeway just east of I-255 to the Gateway Convention Center.

Parking is available at Horseshoe Lake State Park in Granite City, at Gateway Convention Center in Collinsville, at Drost Park in Maryville, and at Hwy 162 at Edwardsville/Troy Road in Troy.

Watershed Trail

Trail Length 5 miles **Surface** Asphalt

The 5 mile Watershed Trail is built along abandoned rail corridor between West Union Street in Edwardsville and northwest to the Watershed Nature Center and Wanda Road in Roxana. There is a 2 mile on-road connection linking the trail to New Poag Road. The trail surface is asphalt.

There is parking on Russell Road and at the Watershed Nature Center on Tower Avenue adjacent to the N.O. Nelson Elementary School in Edwardsville.

Under development is a 7 mile trail connector between the Schoolhouse Trail near Troy to the to the Glen Carbon Heritage Trail, the Nickel Plat Trail, the Nature Trail, the Delyte W. Morris Trail and the Watershed Trail in Edwardsville.

Madison County Trails (continued)

Information   Madison County Transit   (618) 874-7433

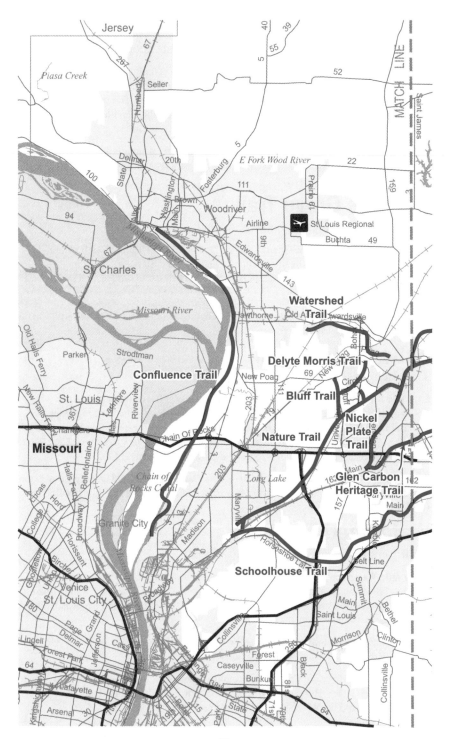

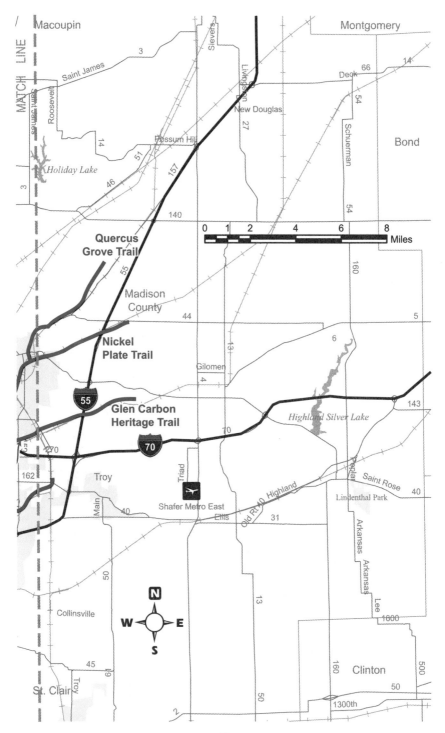

Rockford Area

Information   Rockford Park District
(815) 987-6100
1401 N. Second Street
Rockford, IL 61107-3086

County   Winnebago

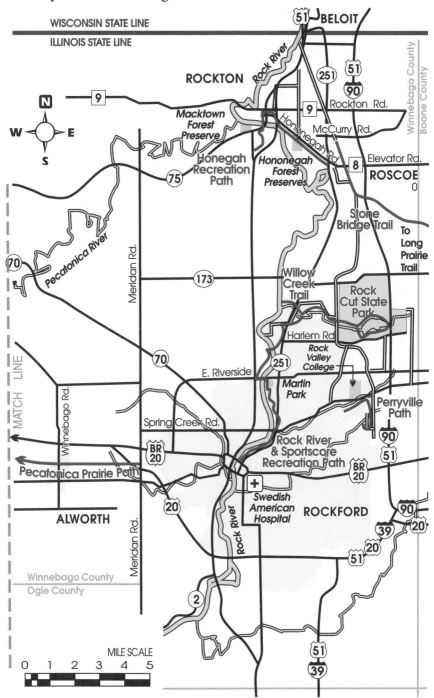

Trails

Algonquin Road Trail

Trail Length	9.5 miles
Surface	Paved
Location & Setting	The Algonquin Trail is located in northwest Cook County. It runs from Harper College west to Potawami Woods at Stover and Palatine Roads. The trail generally parallels Algonquin Road, but there is a 6 mile loop around the parameter of the Paul Douglas Forest Preserve and the Highland Woods Golf Course south of Algonquin Road. The setting is open and urban, and wooded as you enter the Forest Preserve.
Information	Cook County Forest Preserve (708) 366-9420
County	Cook

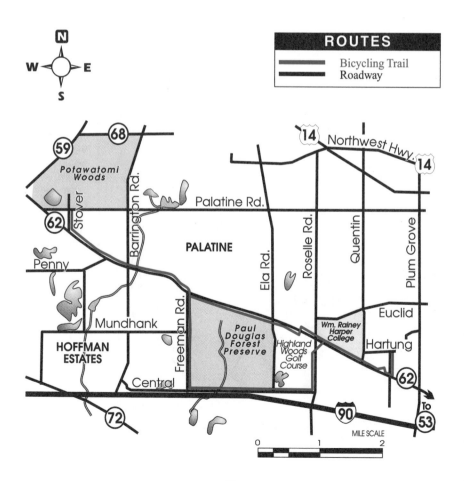

Argyle Lake State Park

Trail Length	7 miles
Surface	Natural – groomed
Location & Setting	From Macomb, west on Rte 136 to Colchester, then north on 500E to the park entrance. Argyle Lake State Park is located about 7 miles west of Macomb, and offers picnicking, camping, and boating in addition to a scenic and rugged 7 mile trail for mountain biking and horseback riding. Effort level is moderate to difficult. There is a concession stand near the boat dock. Class, A, B, C and D campsites are available.
Information	Argyle Lake State Park (309) 776-3422
County	McDonough

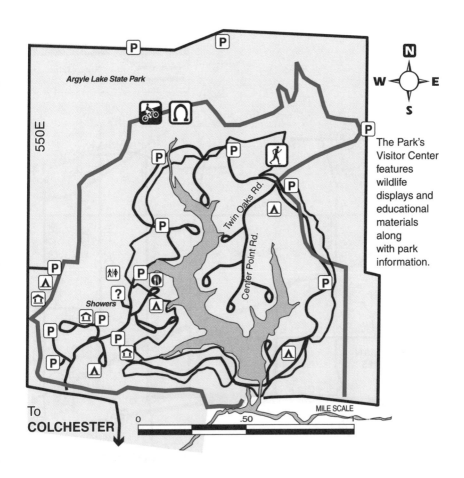

The Park's Visitor Center features wildlife displays and educational materials along with park information.

To COLCHESTER

Arie Crown Bicycle Trail

Trail Length	3.2 miles
Surface	Packed dirt
Location & Setting	Located in south Cook County near Countryside and north of the Palos Forest Preserve. Access at Brainard and Joliet Roads or LaGrange Road, north of 67th Street. Woods, open areas.
Information	Forest Preserve District of Cook County (708) 366-8420
County	Cook

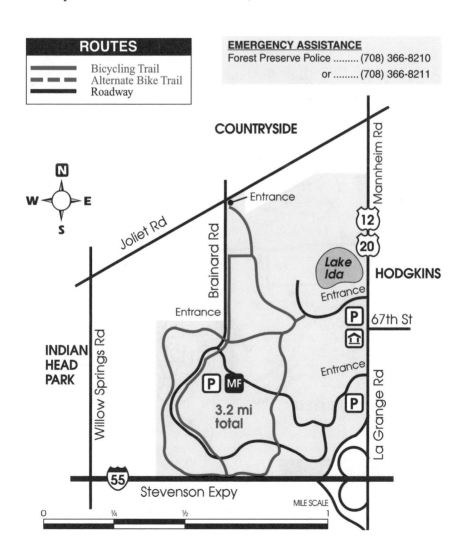

ROUTES

━━━━ Bicycling Trail
╺╸╺╸ Alternate Bike Trail
━━━━ Roadway

EMERGENCY ASSISTANCE
Forest Preserve Police .... (708) 366-8210
or .... (708) 366-8211

COUNTRYSIDE

Mannheim Rd

Entrance

Joliet Rd

Brainard Rd

12
20

Lake Ida

HODGKINS

Entrance

Entrance

P 67th St

Entrance

Willow Springs Rd

INDIAN HEAD PARK

P MF

3.2 mi total

La Grange Rd

P

55

Stevenson Expy

MILE SCALE

0   ¼   ½   1

Blackwell Forest Preserve

Trail Length	7 miles
Surface	Asphalt, limestone screenings, mowed turf
Location & Setting	The Blackwell Preserve, located between Winfield and Warrenville in west central DuPage County, can be accessed from Butterfield Road, 1 mile west of Route 59 or from Mack Road, ¼ miles east of Route 59.
Information	Forest Preserve District of DuPage County (630) 933-7200
County	DuPage

WINFIELD

The Blackwell Preserve has more than 8 miles of multi-purpose trails plus additional footpaths and unmarked trails. The trails lead visitors through a variety of natural settings, including woodlands, marsh and savannas.

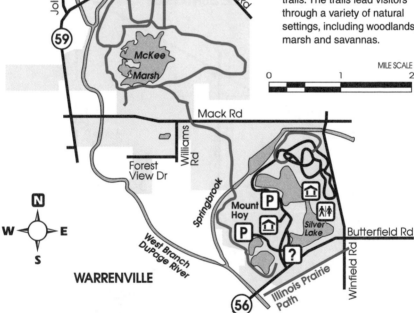

FACILITIES

? Info	♦♦ Restrooms
P Parking	⌂ Shelter
MF Multi Facilities Available	

Refreshments	First Aid	Telephone
Picnic	Restrooms	Lodging

Bicyclists are encouraged to stay on the designated trails in the McKee Marsh area on the north end of the Preserve.

Buffalo Creek Forest Preserve

Trail Length	4 miles
Surface	Crushed granite
Location & Setting	Buffalo Creek is a 396 acre preserve near Buffalo Grove and Long Grove on the southern border of Lake County. The trail runs through open area, crossing several creeks, traversing restored prairies, and skirting the reservoir.
	The trail is about 35 miles northwest of the Chicago loop. From I-294, go west Lake Cook Road for 6 miles to Arlington Heights Road, then north a half mile to Checker Road. Go west on Checker Road to the entrance on the south side of the road.
Information	Lake County Forest Preserves (847) 367-6640
County	Lake

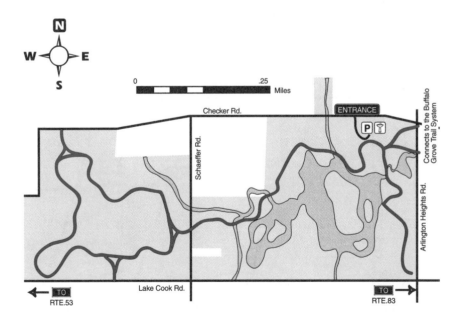

Buffalo Grove Bike Paths

Trail Length	45 miles
Surface	21 miles of asphalt paths & 24 miles of concrete walk
Location & Setting	Buffalo Grove has over 45 miles of multi-use paths, of which 21 miles are 8 to 10 foot wide asphalt, and 24 miles are 8 to 10 foot wide concrete sidewalk. Many of the paths in this urban setting interconnect with its parks, golf courses, and surrounding communities. There is also a connection to the Buffalo Creek Forest Preserve, and a planned connection to the Des Plaines River trail.
	Major access roads into Buffalo Grove are Dundee Road from the south, Milwaukee Avenue from the east, Arlington Heights Road from the west, and Route 45 from the north. Parking near a path is readily available.
Information	Buffalo Grove City Hall (847) 457-2500
County	Lake

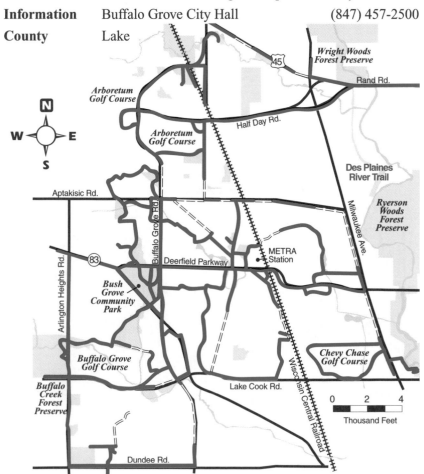

Busse Woods Bicycle Trail

Trail Length	11.2 miles
Surface	Paved
Location & Setting	Located in northwest Cook County in the Ned Brown Preserve, bordered on the north by Arlington Heights and to the east by Elk Grove Village. Wooded areas, open spaces and small lakes.
Information	Forest Preserve District of Cook County (708) 366-9420
County	Cook

The Ned Brown Preserve is a 3,700 acre holding, and surrounds Busse Lake, a 590 acre lake that serves as the focal point of the area.

The bicycle trail winds through the forests and meadows around Busse Lake providing access to many of the preserves unique features.

Trail accesses include Golf Road at Hwy. 90, Arlington Heights Road and Higgins, and at Beisterfield Road and Bisner Road.

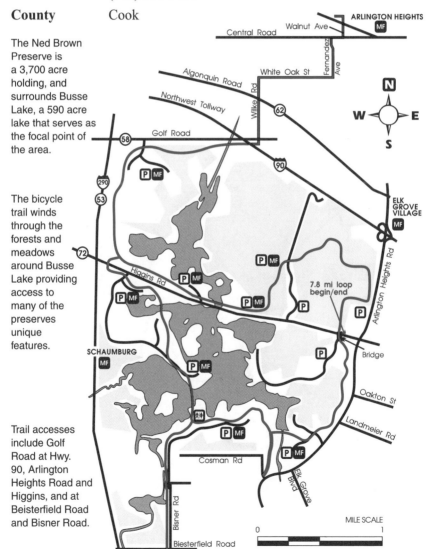

Catlin Park

Trail Length	13 miles
Surface	Natural – groomed
Location & Setting	Catlin Park is an earth and grass system of criss-crossing loop trails located SW of Ottawa and just E of Starved Rock State Park. Effort level is moderate. Facilities include restrooms, picnic areas and fishing ponds.
Information	LaSalle County Parks Dept RR# 2560 E 1251 SR Ottawa, IL 61350
County	LaSalle

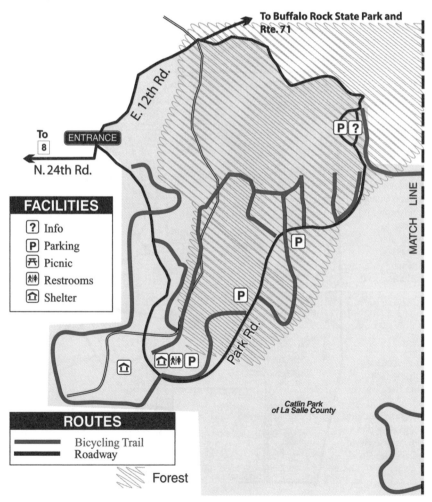

To Buffalo Rock State Park and Rte. 71

E. 12th Rd.

To 8

ENTRANCE

N. 24th Rd.

MATCH LINE

Park Rd.

Catlin Park
of La Salle County

FACILITIES
- [?] Info
- [P] Parking
- [⊼] Picnic
- [⫯⫯] Restrooms
- [⌂] Shelter

ROUTES
- ▬▬ Bicycling Trail
- ▬▬ Roadway
- ⧄⧄ Forest

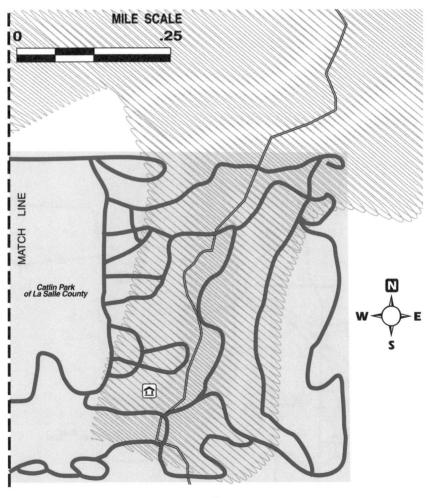

MILE SCALE

0   .25

MATCH LINE

Catlin Park
of La Salle County

N
W ⊕ E
S

Centennial Trail

Trail Length	20 miles - planned
Surface	Crushed Stone
Location & Setting	This planned 20 mile trail runs from the Chicago Portage site at Lyons in Cook County to Lockport in Will County, and forms a link in the Grand Illinois Trail. The surface is crushed limestone and is 10 feet wide. Setting is suburban with most services readily accessible.
Information	Cook County Forest Preserve (708) 336-9420
County	Cook, DuPage, Will

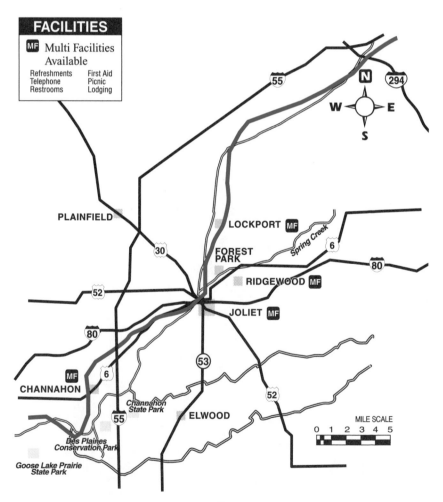

FACILITIES

MF Multi Facilities Available

Refreshments   First Aid
Telephone   Picnic
Restrooms   Lodging

PLAINFIELD

LOCKPORT **MF**

Spring Creek

FOREST PARK

RIDGEWOOD **MF**

JOLIET **MF**

CHANNAHON **MF**

Channahon State Park

ELWOOD

Des Plaines Conservation Park

Goose Lake Prairie State Park

MILE SCALE
0 1 2 3 4 5

Chain O'Lakes State Park

Trail Length	5.0 miles
Surface	Limestone screenings
Location & Setting	Chain O'Lakes State Park is a 2,793 acre park located at the northwest corner of Lake County. Woods, open park areas.
Information	Chain O'Lakes State Park (847) 587-5512
County	Lake

In addition to bicycling, other activities include boating, fishing, picnicking, and camping. Horses and boats can be rented.

ROUTES
- ———— Bicycling Trail
- ▪ ▪ ▪ ▪ Alternate Trail
- ———— Roadway

MILE SCALE
0   ¼   ½   1

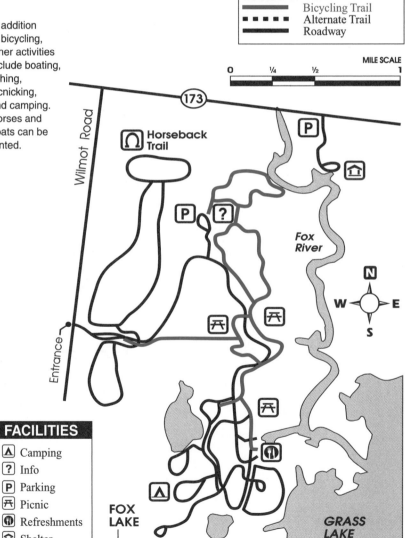

173

Wilmot Road

Horseback Trail

P   ?

Fox River

P

N
W E
S

FACILITIES
- Ⓐ Camping
- ? Info
- Ⓟ Parking
- ⊞ Picnic
- Ⓜ Refreshments
- ⌂ Shelter

FOX LAKE

GRASS LAKE

Chicago Lakefront Bike Path

North Branch to Lakefront Bike Path Connection

FACILITIES

🔧 Bike Repair

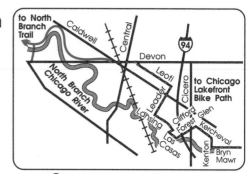

Parking, accesses, restrooms, water, and refreshments located throughout the bikeway.

Northern Section

Trail Length	Approximately 20 miles
Surface	Paved
Location & Setting	From the north, the bike path begins around Bryn Mawr (5600 north) and Sheridan Road, then proceeds south along the shoreline of Lake Michigan to 71st Street. Urban lakefront.
Information	Chicago Park District (312) 747-2200
County	Cook

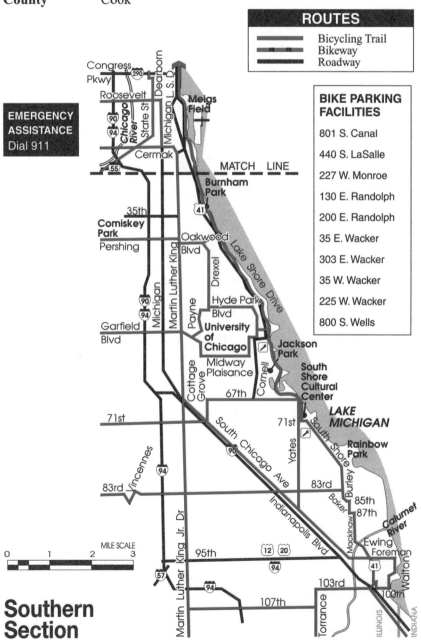

ROUTES

━━━ Bicycling Trail
━━━ Bikeway
━━━ Roadway

EMERGENCY ASSISTANCE
Dial 911

BIKE PARKING FACILITIES

801 S. Canal

440 S. LaSalle

227 W. Monroe

130 E. Randolph

200 E. Randolph

35 E. Wacker

303 E. Wacker

35 W. Wacker

225 W. Wacker

800 S. Wells

Southern Section

Churchill Woods Forest Preserve

Trail Length	2.5 miles
Surface	Screenings, mowed turf
Location & Setting	The 259 acre preserve is located between Lombard and Glen Ellyn in north central DuPage County. Setting is woodlands, prairie and river.
Information	Forest Preserve District of DuPage County (630) 933-7200
County	DuPage

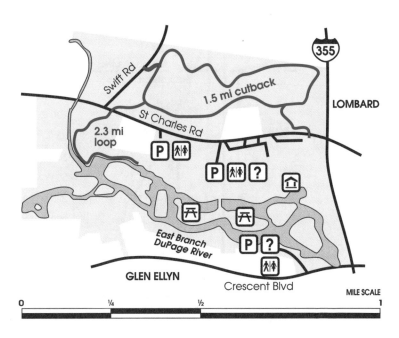

The east branch of the DuPage River provides more than two miles of waterway frontage.

Picnicking is popular and camping facilities are available.

Churchill Wood Forest Preserve offers one of the last native prairies in DuPage County.

ROUTES

 Bicycling Trail
Alternate Use Trail
Roadway

FACILITIES

[?] Info
[P] Parking
[⚘] Picnic
[⚥] Restrooms
[⌂] Shelter

48

Comlara Park

Trail Length	10.5 miles
Surface	Natural turf
Location & Setting	Located in north central Illinois approximately 12 miles north of Bloomington/Normal. The several trails encompass Evergreen Lake. Setting is wooded with lakefront and hills.
Information	McLean County Parks and Recreation (309) 726-2022
County	McLean

No water or restrooms are available on these trails.

From Visitor Center to:
Hwy. 51 .... 2 miles
Normal/Bloomington .... 12 miles

Trails are restricted to single file, are natural turf surface, and are continually changing and variable.

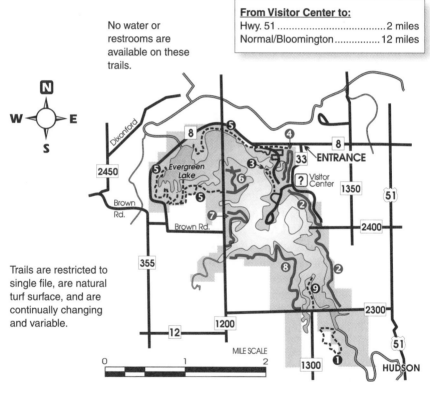

No.	Trail Name	Miles	Effort Level
1.	Shady Hollow Nature Trail *	1.00	Easy
2.	Deer Island Area Access Trail	2.50	Difficult
3.	Hickory Grove Nature Trail *	.50	Easy
4.	Campers Park Access Trail	1.50	Moderate
5.	Lakeview Area Access Trail	3.00	Moderate
6.	White Oak Area Access Trail	.50	Easy
7.	Two Cedars Prairie Access Trail	.50	Easy
8.	Southern Zone Access Trail	2.50	Moderate
9.	Mallard Cove Access Trail *	.25	Moderate

* Foot traffic only

Constitution Trail

Trail Length	15 miles
Surface	Asphalt
Location & Setting	Located in Bloomington and Normal. The trail is mostly built on abandoned railroad bed through parkways in business and residential areas. The north/south segment is wooded with patches of prairie. Trail access from numerous street connections. Picnic tables and benches are located along the trails. Both Illinois State University and Wesleyan University are located within a short distance of the trail.
Information	Bloomington Parks & Recreation Dept (309) 454-9540
County	McClean

ID No. Trailhead   Facilities
1. Atwood Wayside 🟥 HS 🏠 P 🚻 💧 POI
2. Davis Mansion/Jefferson St. Historic Dist. HS POI
3. Historic Franklin Park 🟥 HS P B POI
4. Children's Discovery Museum 🟥 P 🍴 POI
5. Camelback Bridge 🟥 HS B POI
6. Rest Area (Allers Shelter) 🟥 🏠 🚻 B POI
7. Normal Parks & Recreation Office P
8. Normal City Hall Access 🟥 P B
9. Hidden Creek Natural Wayside 🟥 B
10. West Detention Basin 🟥 🏠 P 🚻 B
11. Kerrick Road 🟥 P B
12. Colene Hoose School Access
     Natural Prairie Site 🟥 P POI
13. Audubon Garden B POI
14. Rest Area 🟥 🏠 🚻 B 🍴
15. Natural Prairie Site POI
16. G.E. Road Access P
17. Rest Area, Airport Rd. 🟥 🏠 B
18. Rollingbrook Park 🟥 🏠 P 🚻 B
19. Brookridge Park 🟥 🏠 P 🚻 B
20. Clearwater Park 🟥 🏠 P 🚻 B
21. Bloomington Parks & Recreation Office P
22. Pepper Ridge Park 🟥 🏠 P 🚻 B
23. West Route 9 Wayside P 🚻
24. Alton Depot Park P B
25. Carden Park 🟥 🏠 P 🚻 B 💧

FACILITIES

P	Parking
🟥	Picnic
🍴	Refreshments
🚻	Restrooms
🏠	Shelter
💧	Water
HS	Historical Site
POI	Point of Interest
B	Bench

The trail is built on abandoned trail bed and runs through business and residential areas. The north/south segment is wooded with patches of prairie on the eastern section. Trail accesses from numerous street connections.

Picnic tables and benches are located along the trail. Both Illinois State University and Wesleyan University are located within a short distance of the trail.

Open from dawn to dusk.

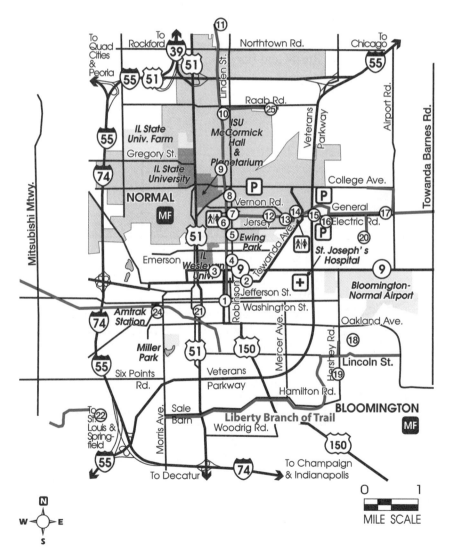

Decatur Area Trails

Decatur

Trail Length	6 miles
Surface	Paved & gravel
Location & Setting	The setting is parkland, lakes, open spaces, and woods. The park is open from 7 am to sunset. The trail winds through Fairview Park, crosses Stevens Creek, through to Kiwanis Park and Sunset Avenue ending at the Rock Springs Environmental Center. It follows the Sangamon River, Lake Decatur, and Stevens Creek.
	Decatur is located in central Illinois west of Springfield on Hwy 32. Parking is available at the Rock Springs Preserve and at Fairview Park. Fairview Park is located at Rte 48 and Hwy 56.
Information	Macon County Conservation District (217) 423-7708
County	Macon

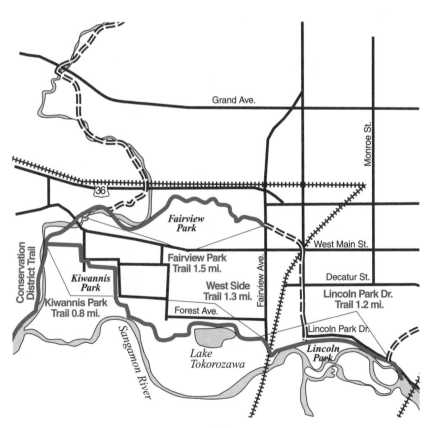

Village of Forsyth

Trail Length   6 miles

Surface   Paved

Location & Setting   The Village of Forsyth is located north of Decatur. The trail system runs through the Village from Forsyth Road south to I-72. Parking is available in the Village Park and on the numerous streets that intersect or parallel the trail.

Information   Macon County Conservation District   (217) 423-7708

County   Macon

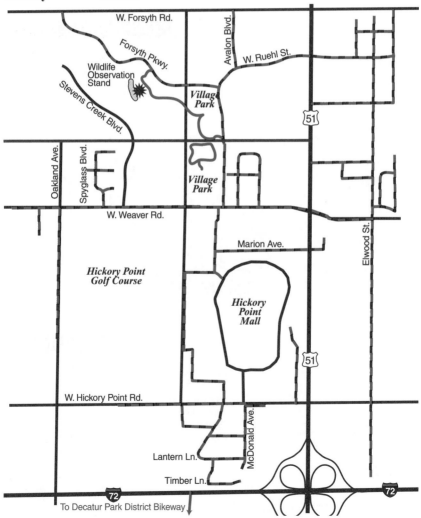

Danada Forest Preserve

Trail Length	2.8 miles of bicycle trails, 3.6 miles total
Surface	Limestone screenings
Location & Setting	Danada Forest Preserve located in the city of Wheaton in central DuPage County, can be accessed from Naperville Road, ½ mile north of Interstate 88. Prairie, woodland, and marsh.
Information	Forest Preserve Dist. of DuPage County (630) 933-7200
County	DuPage

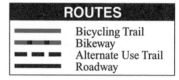

ROUTES

Bicycling Trail
Bikeway
Alternate Use Trail
Roadway

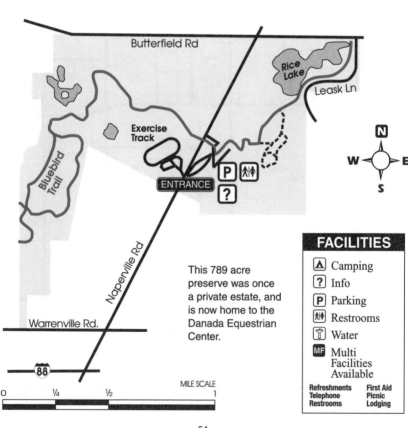

Butterfield Rd

Rice Lake

Leask Ln

Exercise Track

Bluebird Trail

ENTRANCE

P ?

Naperville Rd

Warrenville Rd.

88

This 789 acre preserve was once a private estate, and is now home to the Danada Equestrian Center.

N
W — E
S

FACILITIES

- △ Camping
- ? Info
- P Parking
- 🚻 Restrooms
- 🚰 Water
- MF Multi Facilities Available

Refreshments First Aid
Telephone Picnic
Restrooms Lodging

MILE SCALE
0   ¼   ½   1

Deer Grove Bicycle Trail

Trail Length	4.0 miles
Surface	Paved
Location & Setting	The Deer Grove Preserve consists of rolling upland forest interspersed with wooded ravines and wetlands. Creeks meander through the tract, feeding two lakes located in the preserve. Open spaces, wooded areas (connects to Palatine Trail).
Information	Forest Preserve District of Cook County (708) 366-9420
County	Cook

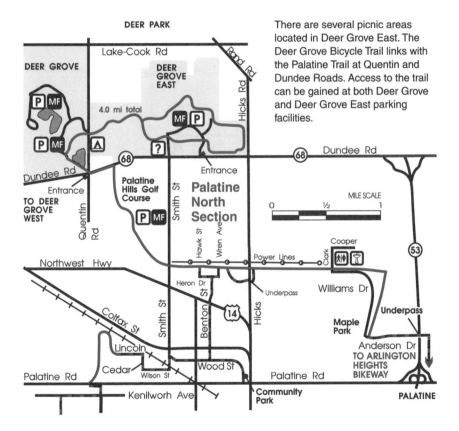

There are several picnic areas located in Deer Grove East. The Deer Grove Bicycle Trail links with the Palatine Trail at Quentin and Dundee Roads. Access to the trail can be gained at both Deer Grove and Deer Grove East parking facilities.

You can ride through a mature forest past a herd of elk, then head for the lake to watch the sailboats. There are six fishing walls if you are inclined to do some fishing along with your bicycling.

Des Plaines Division

Trail Length	12 miles
Surface	Natural groomed (5 to 10 feet wide)
Location & Setting	Located along the east bank of the Des Plaines River in northwest Cook County. It begins at Touhy Avenue, east of Mannheim Road, and continues north to the Lake-Cook County line. The setting is river bottom with woods, open areas and small hills.
Information	Emergency Assistance - Call 911 Cook County Forest Preserve District (708) 366-8420
County	Cook

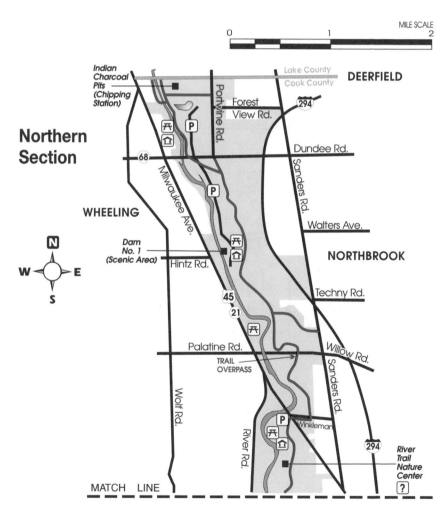

Northern Section

MILE SCALE

DEERFIELD

Indian Charcoal Pits (Chipping Station)

Forest View Rd.

Portwine Rd.

Dundee Rd.

68

Milwaukee Ave.

Sanders Rd.

WHEELING

Walters Ave.

Dam No. 1 (Scenic Area)

NORTHBROOK

Hintz Rd.

45

Techny Rd.

21

Palatine Rd.

Willow Rd.

TRAIL OVERPASS

Sanders Rd.

Wolf Rd.

River Rd.

Winkleman

294

River Trail Nature Center

MATCH LINE

ROUTES

▬▬▬▬ Bicycling Trail
▬ ▬ ▬ Alternate Use Trail
▬▬▬▬ Roadway

FACILITIES

⊞ First Aid
? Info
P Parking
🏮 Picnic
🏠 Shelter

Southern Section

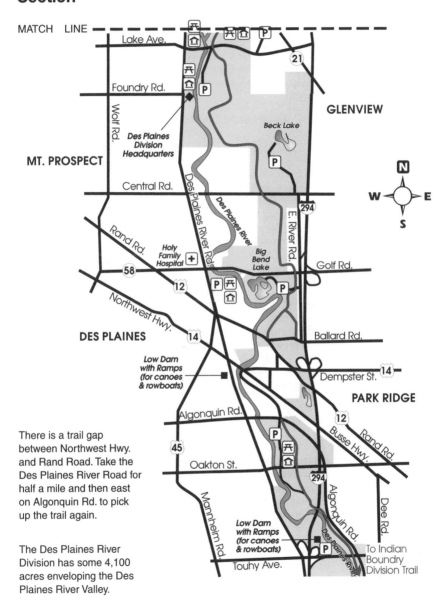

MATCH LINE

Lake Ave.

Foundry Rd.

Wolf Rd.

Des Plaines Division Headquarters

MT. PROSPECT

Central Rd.

GLENVIEW

Beck Lake

Des Plaines River Rd.

Des Plaines River

E. River Rd.

294

Rand Rd.

58

Holy Family Hospital ⊞

12

Big Bend Lake

Golf Rd.

Northwest Hwy.

DES PLAINES

14

Low Dam with Ramps (for canoes & rowboats)

Ballard Rd.

Dempster St. 14

PARK RIDGE

12

Algonquin Rd.

Busse Hwy.

Rand Rd.

45

Oakton St.

294

Algonquin Rd.

Dee Rd.

Mannheim Rd.

Low Dam with Ramps (for canoes & rowboats)

Touhy Ave.

Des Plaines River

To Indian Boundry Division Trail

There is a trail gap between Northwest Hwy. and Rand Road. Take the Des Plaines River Road for half a mile and then east on Algonquin Rd. to pick up the trail again.

The Des Plaines River Division has some 4,100 acres enveloping the Des Plaines River Valley.

Des Plaines River Trail & Greenway

Trail Length	33 miles (49.0 with loops)
Surface	Limestone screenings
Location & Setting	The Des Plaines River Trail parallels its namesake river through Lake County. Open area such as prairies and savannas are common. As you travel through this river valley, look for changes in the landscape. In northern Lake County, the valley is wide and the river meanders. In southern Lake County, the valley is narrow and the river runs a straighter course. Woodlands are more common.
Information	Lake County Forest Preserves (847) 367-6640
County	Lake

From Lake Cook Road you'll travel 1.8 miles before reaching a current 2 mile gap between Estonia & Riverside Road. From Riverside Road the trail continues north, passing through Half Day and Wright Woods Forest Preserves, then MacArthur Woods, Old School Forest Preserves and finally past Sterling Lake before ending at Russell Road at the Wisconsin State line.

ROUTES

▬▬▬	Bicycling Trail
▬▪▬▪	Bikeway
▬ ▬ ▬	Alternate Bike Trail
═ ═ ═	Planned Trail
▬▬▬	Roadway

Lake County Forest Preserves

Open daily from 8 am to sunset daily. Alcoholic beverages may not be consumed in or near parking areas. Pets are permitted, except in picnic areas, but must be controlled on a leash (no longer than 10 feet). Forest Preserve Ranger Police regularly patrol the Preserves. Ranger Police receive the same basic training as other Illinois police officers and have the same authority.

More than 25,000 acres make up the Lake County Forest Preserves, a dynamic and unique system of natural and cultural resources.

FACILITIES

[?]	Info
[P]	Parking
[丙]	Picnic
[❿]	Refreshments
[♟♟]	Restrooms
[🏠]	Shelter
[💧]	Water

Van Patten Woods consists of 972 acres. Enjoy picnic areas, reserveable shelters and shoreline fishing at 74 acre Sterling Lake.

Right-of-Way Laws

When you come to a stop sign at a two-way stop intersection, remember that the traffic on the cross street has the right-of-way. You must yield the right-of-way to pedestrians and vehicles on the cross street before you go ahead.

Blind, hearing impaired or physically handicapped persons can be identified by their white canes, support or guide dogs. You must always yield the right-of-way to them.

If a policeman directs otherwise, the right-of-way laws do not apply and riders and pedestrians must do as the officer tells them.

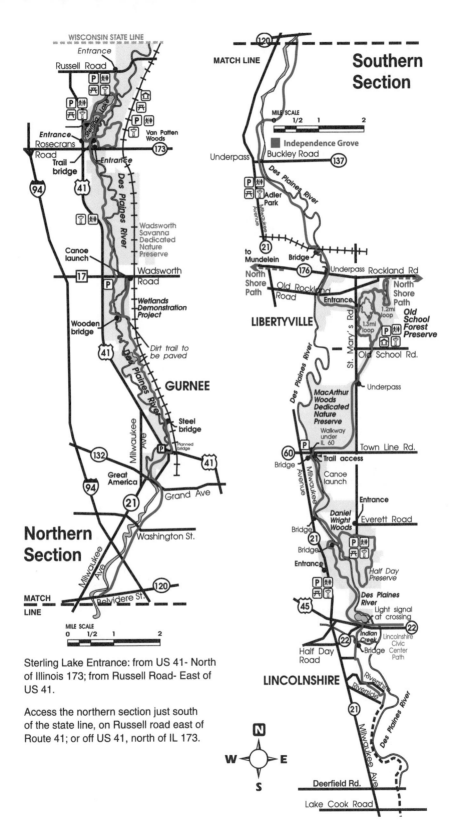

WISCONSIN STATE LINE

Entrance
Russell Road

Entrance
Rosecrans Road
Trail bridge
Entrance

Van Patten Woods

Des Plaines River

Wadsworth Savanna Dedicated Nature Preserve

Canoe launch

Wadsworth Road

Wetlands Demonstration Project

Wooden bridge

Dirt trail to be paved

GURNEE

Steel bridge

Planned bridge

Great America

Grand Ave

Washington St.

Northern Section

MATCH LINE

Belvidere St.

MILE SCALE
0   1/2   1   2

Sterling Lake Entrance: from US 41- North of Illinois 173; from Russell Road- East of US 41.

Access the northern section just south of the state line, on Russell road east of Route 41; or off US 41, north of IL 173.

Southern Section

MATCH LINE

MILE SCALE
0   1/2   1   2

■ Independence Grove

Buckley Road

Underpass

Des Plaines River

Adler Park

Milwaukee Avenue

to Mundelein

Bridge

Underpass   Rockland Rd.

North Shore Path

Old Rockland Road

Entrance

North Shore Path

1.2mi loop

1.3mi loop

Old School Forest Preserve

LIBERTYVILLE

St. Mary's Rd.

Old School Rd.

Underpass

MacArthur Woods Dedicated Nature Preserve

Walkway under IL 60

Town Line Rd.

Trail access

Canoe launch

Bridge

Milwaukee Avenue

Entrance

Daniel Wright Woods

Everett Road

Bridge

Bridge

Entrance

Half Day Preserve

Des Plaines River

Light signal at crossing

Half Day Road

Indian Creek

Lincolnshire Civic Center Path

Bridge

LINCOLNSHIRE

Riverside

Des Plaines River

N
W — E
S

Deerfield Rd.

Lake Cook Road

59

Edward R. Madigan State Park

Trail Length	7 miles
Surface	Natural
Location & Setting	This is a scenic 7 mile hiking/biking trail, which meanders through grasses, trees and creek bottoms. The Park is situated on the southern edge of Lincoln, and surrounds the Lincoln Correctional Center and Logan Correctional Center. Facilities include picnic areas and a canoe access to Salt Creek.
	From Lincoln, southwest on Rte 66 to the Park entrance on the left. From Springfield, go north on Hwy 55 to Rte 66, then east to the Park.
Information	Edward R. Madigan State Park (217) 735-2424
County	Logan

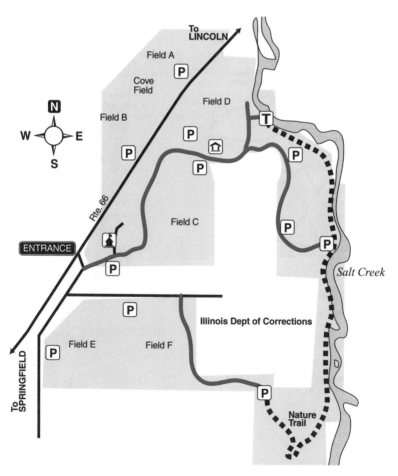

Evanston Bike Paths/ North Shore Channel

Trail Length	7.0 miles	
Surface	Paved	
Location & Setting	City of Evanston in northeast Cook County north of Chicago and bordering Lake Michigan. Setting is urban, North Shore Channel is open park area.	
Information	Evanston Chamber of Commerce	(847) 328-1500
County	Cook	

EVANSTON-
LAKE SHORE
PATH TO GREEN
BAY TRAIL

Lincoln St. west
to Ashland
(1 mi.)

Ashland north to
Isabella
(.4 mi.)

Isabella west to
Poplar Dr.
(.4 mi.)

Poplar Dr. north
to Forest Ave.
(1 mi.)

EMERGENCY
ASSISTANCE

Dial 911

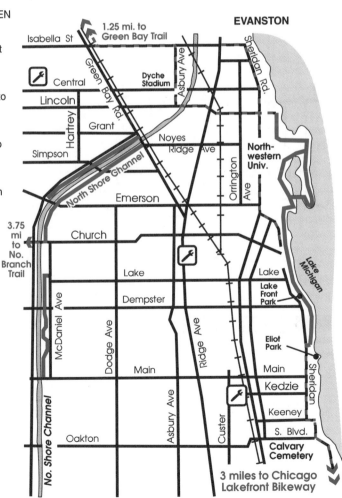

Fermilab Bike Trail

Trail Length	4.0 miles
Surface	Paved
Location & Setting	The east access is off Batavia Road just west of Hwy. 59. The west access is off Kirk Road about ¾ miles north of Butterfield Road. Tall grass prairie, flood plain woods and wetlands.
Information	Fermilab Prairie Path Volunteers (630) 840-3351
County	DuPage

As an alternate, tour the scenic 4 mile trail through Fermilab, or extend it to a 14 mile round trip by way of the Aurora Branch, Batavia Spur and paved paths along Kirk Road and Batavia Road.

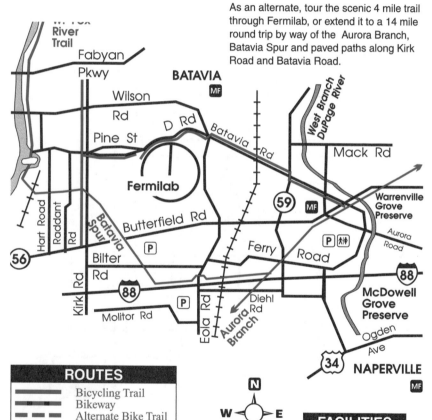

You can learn about everything from subatomic particles to bison at Fermilab. Built in the 1950's, Fermilab is on the cutting edge of particle acceleration research. However, don't miss the woods, ponds, and prairie. The top floor (15th) is open for observation, and can provide a spectacular view of the Fox Valley.

Fullersburg Forest Preserve

Trail Length	3.8 miles
Surface	Screenings, asphalt
Location & Setting	Located between Oak Brook and Hinsdale in east central DuPage County, Fullersburg Forest Preserve can be accessed from Spring Road, ½ mile northwest of York Road. Woodlands, prairie, creek crossings.
Information	Forest Preserve District of DuPage County (630) 933-7200
County	Du Page

Fullersburg Woods, with 221 acres, is a nature sanctuary for plants and animals. It has a Visitors and Environmental Center which is open daily from 9am to 5pm.

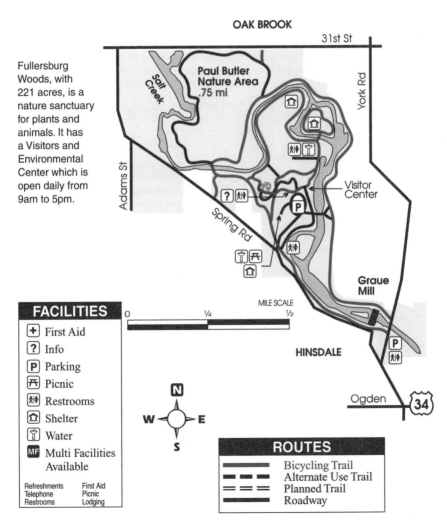

FACILITIES

- ✚ First Aid
- ? Info
- P Parking
- ⛩ Picnic
- 🚻 Restrooms
- 🏠 Shelter
- 🚰 Water
- MF Multi Facilities Available

Refreshments	First Aid
Telephone	Picnic
Restrooms	Lodging

ROUTES

———	Bicycling Trail
▬ ▬ ▬	Alternate Use Trail
≡ ≡ ≡	Planned Trail
———	Roadway

Fox River Trail

Trail Length	41.7 miles
Surface	Paved, limestone screenings
Location & Setting	Follows the Fox River between Crystal Lake and Aurora. Open spaces and small communities.
Information	Fox Valley Park District (630) 897-0516
	Dundee Township Tourist Center (847) 426-2255
County	McHenry, Kane

Northward from Oswego, this trail winds through the Fox River Valley running northward from Aurora to Crystal Lake. You'll bike through forest and nature preserves, and several historic and interesting communities. This popular trail connects the Illinois Prairie Path to the east, to the Great Western Trail west of St. Charles and to the Virgil Gilman Trail in Aurora. Plans include extending the trail via bikeways through Crystal Lake, then connecting to the Prairie Trail (north section) which will continue to the Wisconsin state line.

Red Oak Nature Center is a 40 acre oak and maple forest on the east bank of the Fox River. Inside the nature center building, you'll find a contemporary museum stressing the four basic elements of life...sun, air, water and soil.

Devil's Cave is one of the most unusual natural features on the trail. Although small, this is one of the very few caves in northeastern Illinois. Rich in folklore, this cave is believed to have been used by the Pottawatomie Indians.

FACILITIES

- 🔧 Bike Repair
- ✚ First Aid
- ❓ Info
- 🛏 Lodging
- 🅿 Parking
- 🌳 Picnic
- 🍴 Refreshments
- 🚻 Restrooms
- 🏠 Shelter
- **MF** Multi Facilities Available

Refreshments   First Aid
Telephone   Picnic
Restrooms   Lodging

ROUTES

Bicycling Trail
Alternate Bike Trail
Roadway

ROUTE SLIP	SEGMENT	TOTAL
Crystal Lake Ave – Crystal Lake	0	
Botz Rd - Carpentersville	7.0	7.0
Hwy 72/68 – E. Dundee	4.0	11.0
Hwy 90 – Elgin	3.5	14.5
Hwy 20 – Elgin	5.1	19.6
River Crossing – S. Elgin	2.9	22.5
Army Trail Rd – St. Charles	4.7	27.2
State St. – Geneva	5.0	32.2
Hwy 88	7.5	39.5
Illinois Ave. – Aurora	2.0	41.5
River Crossing – Oswego	7.5	49.0

For information concerning trail activities, please contact:
Illinois Department of Natural Resources Office of Resource
Marketing and Education
524 S. Second St.
Springfield, IL 62701-1787
(217)782-7454

Northern Section

Southern Section

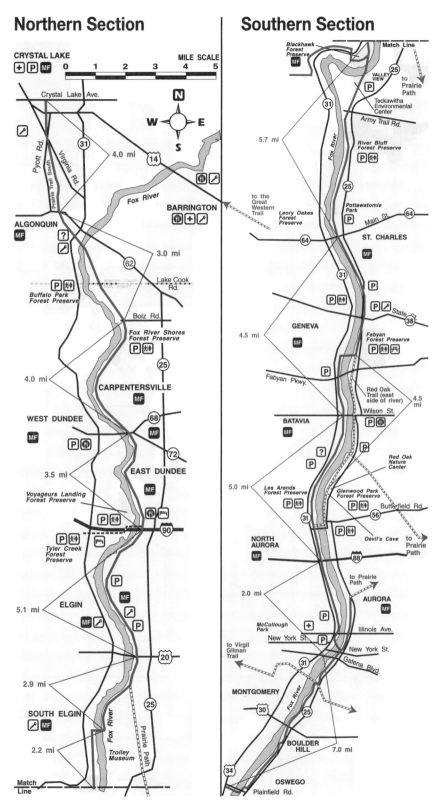

CRYSTAL LAKE

MILE SCALE
0 1 2 3 4 5

N
W E
S

Crystal Lake Ave.

Pyott Rd.
Virginia Rd.
Prairie Trail South
31

4.0 mi
14

Fox River

BARRINGTON

ALGONQUIN

3.0 mi

62

Lake Cook Rd.

Buffalo Park
Forest Preserve

Bolz Rd.

Fox River Shores
Forest Preserve

25

4.0 mi

CARPENTERSVILLE

68

WEST DUNDEE

72

3.5 mi

EAST DUNDEE

Voyageurs Landing
Forest Preserve

90

Tyler Creek
Forest Preserve

ELGIN

5.1 mi

20

2.9 mi

25

SOUTH ELGIN

2.2 mi

Fox River

Prairie Path

Trolley
Museum

Match
Line

Blackhawk
Forest
Preserve

Match Line

VALLEY
VIEW

25

to
Prairie
Path

31

Teckawitha
Environmental
Center

Army Trail Rd.

5.7 mi

Fox River

River Bluff
Forest Preserve

25

to the
Great
Western
Trail

Leory Oakes
Forest
Preserve

Pottawatomie
Park

64

Main St.

64

ST. CHARLES

31

State St.
38

4.5 mi

GENEVA

Fabyan
Forest Preserve

Fabyan Pkwy.

Red Oak
Trail (east
side of river)

4.5
mi

Wilson St.

BATAVIA

Red Oak
Nature
Center

5.0 mi

Les Arends
Forest Preserve

Glenwood Park
Forest Preserve

Butterfield Rd.

56

31

Devil's Cave

to
Prairie
Path

**NORTH
AURORA**

88

to Prairie
Path

2.0 mi

AURORA

McCullough
Park

Illinois Ave.

New York St.

New York St.

to Virgil
Gilman
Trail

31

Galena Blvd.

MONTGOMERY

30

Fox River

25

**BOULDER
HILL**

7.0 mi

34

OSWEGO

Plainfield Rd.

Fulton Bike Trail (F.A.S.T.)

Trail Length	6 miles existing, 8+ miles planned
Surface	Asphalt, shared streets
Location & Setting	Located in Fulton along the Mississippi River in northwest Illinois. Setting is riverfront, city streets.
Information	Fulton Chamber of Commerce (815) 589-4545
County	Whiteside

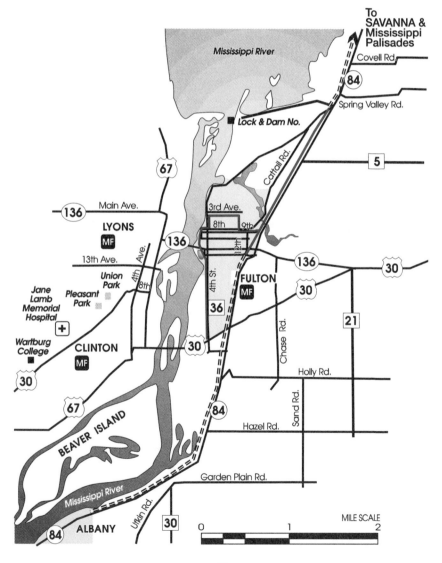

Grant Woods Forest Preserve

Trail Length	6.0 miles
Surface	Limestone screenings
Location & Setting	Grant Woods is east of Fox Lake and bounded by Rte. 59 on the west, Rte. 83 on the east, Rte. 132 north and Rte. 134 south. Enter on Monaville Rd. east of Rte. 59. The northern half is largely marsh and prairie.
Information	Lake County Forest Preserve (847) 367-6640
County	Lake

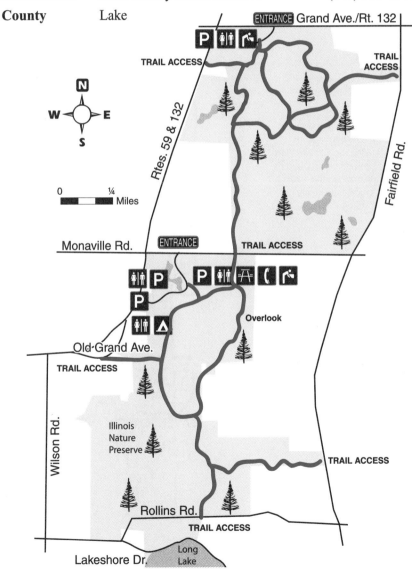

Grand Illinois Trail

Trail Length	475 miles
Location & Setting	Existing and planned trails forming a loop of northern Illinois, from the suburbs of Chicago to the Mississippi and from the Wisconsin border to the I & M Canal.
Information	Illinois Department of Conservation (217) 782-3715
	Illinois Trails Conservancy (815) 569-2472
County	Covers 16 counties

A series of 17 trails and road segments covering several hundred miles looping Northern Illinois. Some of the proposed route is still conceptual, with linkages to trails via lightly traveled roads and streets.

ROUTES

——	Bicycling Trail
-■-■-	Bikeway Incomplete
——	Roadway

GRAND ILLINOIS TRAIL SYSTEM SEGMENTS

1. Local roads
2. Pecatonica Trail
3. Rockford Area Trails
4. Stone Bridge and Long Prairie Trails
5. Conceptual connection
6. Crystal Lake/Harvard Trail segment
7. Prairie Trail segment
8. Fox River Trail segment
9. Illinois Prairie Path segment
10. Des Plaines River Trail segment
11. Centennial Trail
12. Lockport Historical & Joliet Heritage Trails (& roads)
13. Illinois and Michigan (I & M) Canal State Trail segment
14. Conceptual connection
15. Hennepin Canal State Trail segment
16. Conceptual connection
17. Great River Trail

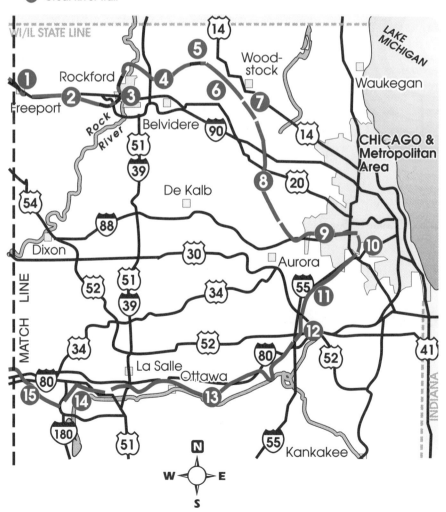

Great Western Trail

Trail Length	18 miles
Surface	Limestone screenings
Location & Setting	This 18 mile trail extends from the LeRoy Oakes Forest Preserve west of St. Charles to Sycamore at Old State and Airport Road in Kane and DeKalb counties and stands on the former site of the Chicago and Northwestern Railroad line. Rural landscape, wetlands, farmlands, small communities.
Information	Kane County Forest Preserve (630) 232-5980
County	DeKalb, Kane

There is a bike route from the city of DeKalb to a nature trail. The Peace Road Trail links DeKalb and Sycamore with a recreational path.

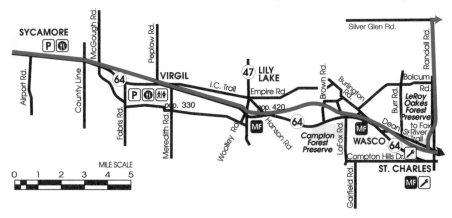

ROUTES

▬▬▬	Bicycling Trail
▬▬▬	Roadway

There are plans to provide a 3.5 mile corridor between the Fox River Trail and the Great Western Trail. The path will run south from Silver Glen Road along Randall Road on a county highway easement to LeRoy Oakes Forest Preserve, where it will connect with the Great Western Trail.

FACILITIES

🔧	Bike Repair
?	Info
🏠	Lodging
P	Parking
🎪	Picnic
🍴	Refreshments
🚻	Restrooms
MF	Multi Facilities Available

Refreshments   First Aid
Telephone   Picnic
Restrooms   Lodging

The Great Western Trail is a rail-to-trails conversion. Horseback riding is permitted from Lily Lake to LeRoy Oakes. Snowmobiling is permitted with 4 or more inches of snow.

Green Bay Trail

Trail Length	6.0 miles
Surface	Paved
Location & Setting	From Wilmette to the Lake County line, running mostly parallel to the Chicago and Northwestern rail line. Urban setting.
Information	Winnetka Park District (847) 501-2040
County	Cook

FACILITIES

🔧 Bike Repair
🅿 Parking
MF Multi Facilities Available

Refreshments   First Aid
Telephone   Picnic
Restrooms   Lodging

ROUTES

━━━ Bicycling Trail
━━━ Roadway

This mainly urban to suburban setting provides ample opportunities to enjoy the many eating establishments and beautiful homes along the trail. The south trailhead (Forest Ave. in Wilmette) is 1.2 mi. west of Sheridan Rd. and 2.5 mi. east of I-90/94.

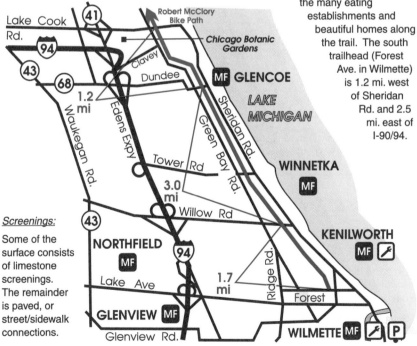

Screenings:

Some of the surface consists of limestone screenings. The remainder is paved, or street/sidewalk connections.

GLENCOE
- Scott Ave. & Harbor St. (.4 mi.)
- South Ave. & Hazel Ave. (.2 mi.)
- Maple Hill Rd. & Ravinia Park (1.1 mi.)

MILE SCALE

0   1   2

Great River Trail
Ben Butterworth Pathway

Trail Length	62.0 miles
Surface	Paved paths (10 feet), shared streets, undeveloped
Location & Setting	The Great River Trail will eventually run from Rock Island to the Mississippi Palisades State Park, north of Savanna, along the Mississippi River in northwest Illinois. The setting is riverfront, urban to small communities, rural, woods, open areas, farmland.

Information	Bi-State Regional Commission	(309) 793-6300
	Parks & Recreation Dept.	(309) 752-1573
	Hampton Village Hall	(309) 755-7165
County	Rock Island, Whiteside, Carroll	

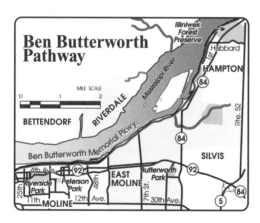

ROUTES
▬▬▬ Bicycling Trail
═ ═ ═ Planned Trail
▬▬▬ Roadway

Always lock your bicycle when it is parked. Register your bicycle with your local police department if possible. Be sure to keep your bike's serial number in a safe place.

If you are uncertain of the condition of your bicycle, visit a local bike shop. Most shops offer free safety inspections and books on do-it-yourself maintenance.

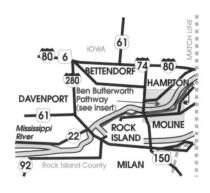

Trailheads

Rock Island	Sunset Park, 18th Avenue and IL Route 92
East Moline	Waterfront & Mississippi Parks (north sides of city)
Hampton	Riverfront Park (south side), Illiniwek Park (north side)
Rapids City	Shuler's Shady Grove Park
Port Byron	Boat access area
Albany	Boat access area
Thomson	Downtown area, Thomson Causeway, Buck's Barn
Savanna	Downtown area
	Mississippi Palisades State Park

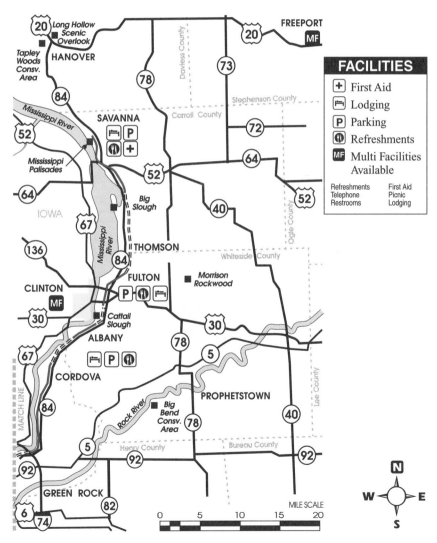

FACILITIES

- ✚ First Aid
- ⌷ Lodging
- P Parking
- ⓜ Refreshments
- **MF** Multi Facilities Available

Refreshments   First Aid
Telephone   Picnic
Restrooms   Lodging

Green Belt Forest Preserve

Trail Length	4.0 miles of looped trails
Surface	Crushed gravel
Location & Setting	The Greenbelt Forest Preserve is nestled between the cities of Waukegan and North Chicago, east of Route 41 and south of Route 120.
Information	Lake County Forest Preserve (847) 367-6640
County	Lake

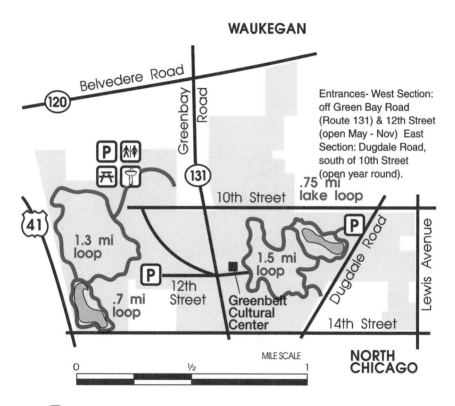

WAUKEGAN

Belvedere Road

120

Greenbay Road

131

Entrances- West Section: off Green Bay Road (Route 131) & 12th Street (open May - Nov) East Section: Dugdale Road, south of 10th Street (open year round).

10th Street

.75 mi lake loop

41

1.3 mi loop

1.5 mi loop

12th Street

.7 mi loop

Greenbelt Cultural Center

Dugdale Road

Lewis Avenue

14th Street

MILE SCALE

0   ½   1

NORTH CHICAGO

N
W — E
S

FACILITIES

P	Parking
🏞	Picnic
🚻	Restrooms
🏠	Shelter
💧	Water

ROUTES

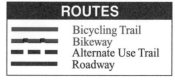

——	Bicycling Trail
- ■-	Bikeway
– – –	Alternate Use Trail
——	Roadway

Greene Valley Forest Preserve

Trail Length	10.0 miles
Surface	Gravel, mowed turf
Location & Setting	Greene Valley Forest Preserve is located in far south central DuPage County, on Greene Road, ½ mile south of 75th Street. 1,400 acres of woodlands and grasslands.
Information	Forest Preserve District of DuPage County (630) 933-7200
County	DuPage

Trails are symbol coded and may be traveled in both directions. Loop trails range from 1.75 to 6.25 miles.

Access on:
Thunderbird Road
70th Street
Greene Road between Hobson Road and 75th Street.

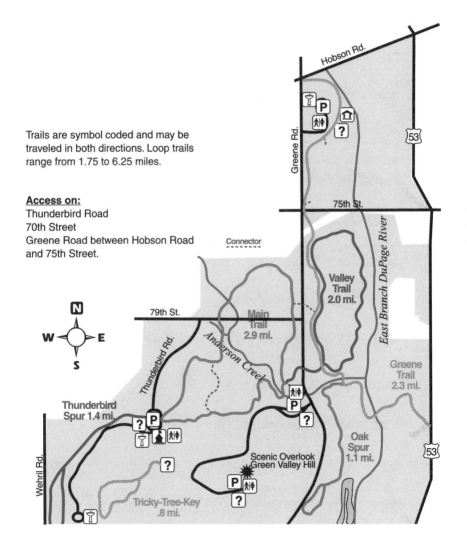

Heartland Pathways

Trail Length	33 miles
Surface	Ballast
Location & Setting	An abandoned railbed that runs from Clinton to Seymour in east central Illinois. Its 100 foot wide corridor contains one of the last remnants of tall grass prairies in Illinois.
Information	Heartland Pathways (217) 351-1911
County	DeWitt, Pratt, Champaign

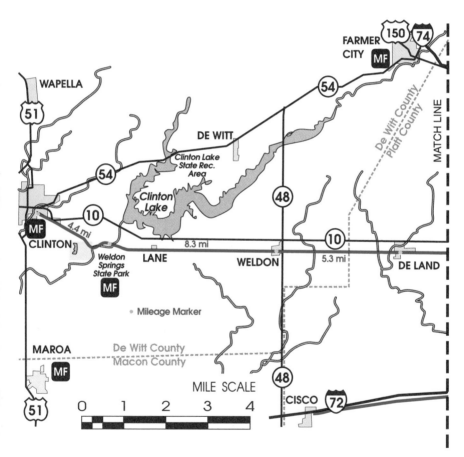

Access can be achieved at connecting roads. There is no designated parking.

FACILITIES

+ First Aid

MF Multi Facilities
Available

Refreshments	First Aid
Telephone	Picnic
Restrooms	Lodging

The Heartland Pathways promotes the observation and conservation of the natural and cultural landscapes of Illinois.

ROUTES

Bicycling Trail
Alternate Use Trail
Roadway

Points of interests include a railroad museum in Monticello and the Allerton Park country estate with its formal gardens, statuary, pools and hiking trails, just west of Monticello.

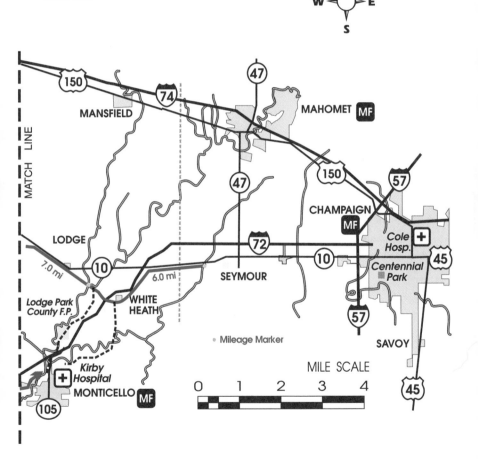

Hennepin Canal Parkway

Trail Length	98 miles
Surface	Bituminous – 2 miles, oil & chip – 61 miles, gravel – 35 miles
Location & Setting	The Hennepin Canal Parkway is a unique linear waterway corridor in northwestern Illinois. The main line of the waterway extends from the great bend of the Illinois River to the Mississippi River, west of Milan.
Information	Illinois Dept. of Natural Resources (815) 454-2328
County	Bureau, Henry, Lee Rock Island, Whiteside.

There are plans to add six miles of trail to connect the Great River Trail along the Mississippi River to the Hennepin Canal Trail.

ROUTES

▬▬▬	Bicycling Trail
▬▬▬	Roadway

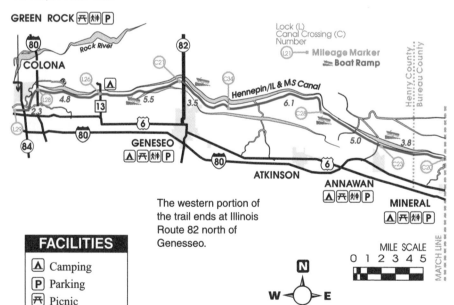

GREEN ROCK 🎪👫P

COLONA

Rock River

Lock (L)
Canal Crossing (C)
Number
Mileage Marker
Boat Ramp

Hennepin/IL & MS Canal

Henry County
Bureau County

GENESEO
🏕🎪👫P

ATKINSON

ANNAWAN
🏕🎪👫P

MINERAL
🏕🎪👫P

The western portion of the trail ends at Illinois Route 82 north of Genesseo.

FACILITIES

🏕	Camping
P	Parking
🎪	Picnic
👫	Restrooms
MF	Multi Facilities Available

Refreshments	First Aid
Telephone	Picnic
Restrooms	Lodging

MILE SCALE
0 1 2 3 4 5

MATCH LINE

N
W — E
S

There are 33 locks on the canal. The canal was completed in 1907, but was only used for a short while before being replaced by the railroad.

78

The parkway is a popular recreatonal area for pleasure boating, picnicking, primitive camping, horseback riding, snowmobiling, backpacking, and hiking in addition to bicycling. A feeder from the Rock River connects to the main line between Sheffield and Mineral. There are numerous parking areas and road accesses along the parkway.

Day-use facilities consists of picnic tables, pit toilets and parking areas. Most of the areas along the canal have these facilities:

Toilets: Locks 11, 17, 21, 22, 23, 24 and bridges 14, 15, 23 and Visitor Center are have toilet facilities.
Water: Drinking water is available at Locks 21, 22 and the Visitor Center area.
Visitor Center: Includes information, displays, flush toilets, drinking water, playground equipment, picnic areas, boat launching ramp & marina.

The parkway extends south 29.3 miles along the feeder canal. Just north of Interstate 80, midway between Routes 78 and 40, the feeder meets the main canal. From this point the parkway runs southwest 46.9 miles to the Mississippi River near Rock Island and southeast 28.4 miles to the Illinois River near the town of Hennepin.

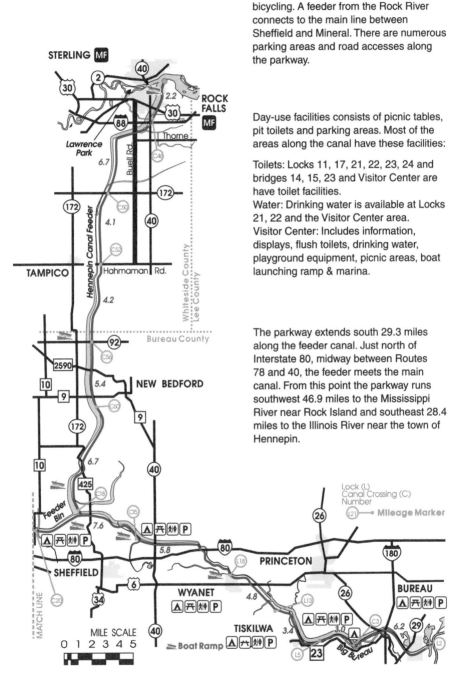

Herrick Lake Forest Preserve

Trail Length	6.5 miles
Surface	Limestone screenings
Location & Setting	Located in central DuPage County, between Winfield and Naperville. Access from Herrick Road or Butterfield Road. Herrick Lake has 760 acres with a 21 acre lake.
Information	Forest Preserve District of DuPage County (630) 933-7200
County	DuPage

WINFIELD

WHEATON

Weisbrook Rd.

Orchard Rd.

Butterfield Rd. — 56

Herrick Rd.

Arrowhead Golf Course
Wheaton Park District

56

To Danada Forest Preserve

WARRENVILLE

Park Ranger

Meadowlark Trail

Galusha Ave.

Bluebird Trail

Warrenville Rd.

Green Heron Trail

Mill St.

Indian Hill Dr.

Naperville Rd.

88

88

Diehl

NAPERVILLE

MILE SCALE

0   ½   1

There is a concession building on the eastern shore of the lake. Canoes and row boats are available for rental.

Hononegah Recreation Path

Trail Length	2.5 miles
Surface	Asphalt
Location & Setting	The path runs along the south side of Hononegah Road between Hwy. 251 and proceeds northwest ¼ mile west of Route 2. Open area with small communities at either end.
Information	Rockford Park District (815) 987-8865
County	Winnebago

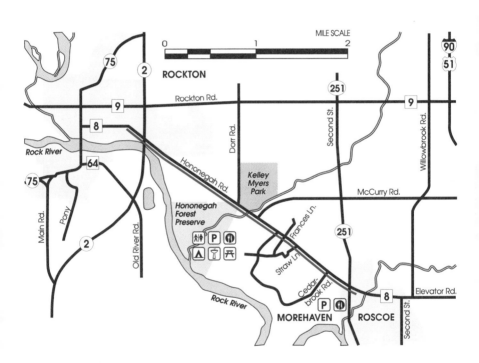

FACILITIES

- 🏕 Camping
- ❓ Info
- 🅿 Parking
- 🌲 Picnic
- 🍴 Refreshments
- 🚻 Restrooms
- 🏠 Shelter
- 🚰 Water

ROUTES

Bicycling Trail
Roadway

I & M Canal State Trail

Trail Length	56 miles
Surface	Limestone screenings
Location & Setting	In northeast Illinois, the eastern trailhead begins at the Channanon access. The trail proceeds west to the city of LaSalle, where there are multiple access points and parking. Rural landscape, prairie, small communities
Information	I & M Canal State Trail (815) 942-9501
County	Will, Grundy, LaSalle

BUFFALO ROCK STATE PARK

Directions: Boyce Memorial Drive south to Ottawa Avenue. West 1.8 miles, past Naplate, to the park entrance. Located five miles from the Fox River Aqueduct on the north bank of the Illinois River. Atop the sandstone bluff at the summit of Buffalo Rock is a sweeping view of the Illinois River. It has several picnic areas

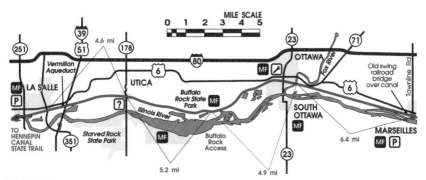

LA SALLE—
Parking off Canal St. one half block south of Joliet St.

OTTAWA—
Sight of the first Lincoln-Douglas Debate, Reddick Mansion, Fox River Aqueduct and other historic attractions.

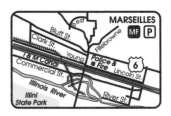

One of the largest earth sculptures ever built, the Effigy Tumuli is located near the park. This reclaimed mine site has turned a barren wasteland into an area filled with recreational opportunities and interesting landscapes. It contains five large earthen figures (effigies) of native aquatic animals. Represented in geometric forms are a water strider, frog, catfish, turtle and a snake.

Bicyclists can take advantage of the groomed towpath to enjoy the natural and manmade wonders. The trail is marked and has various wayside exhibits that describe features of the canal era.

The I&M (Illinois and Michigan) Canal provided the first complete water route from the east coast to the Gulf of Mexico by connecting Lake Michigan to the Mississippi River by way of the Illinois River.

[handwritten note: rode on 5-27-06 from LaSalle past to a little — navi caused mud but otherwise pretty scenery.]

AUX SABLE—
This access area is eight miles from Channahon where an aqueduct, lock and locktender's house can be found.

CHANNANON ACCESS—
Exit Hwy. 6 at Canal St. Proceed one half mile southeast to Story St., then one block west.

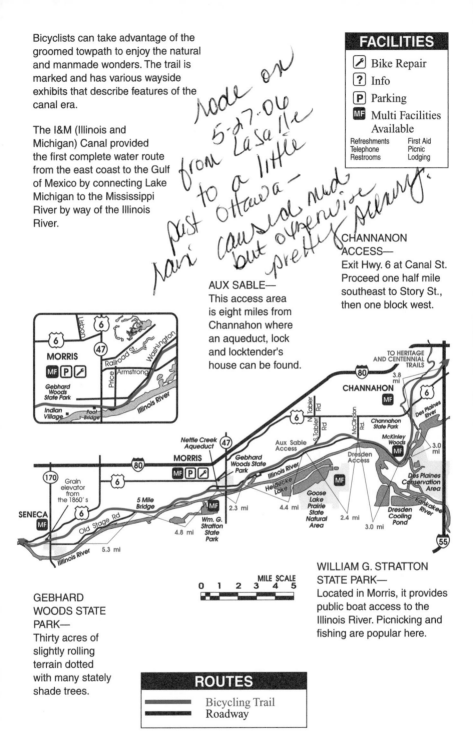

MILE SCALE
0 1 2 3 4 5

ROUTES

━━━ Bicycling Trail
━━━ Roadway

GEBHARD WOODS STATE PARK—
Thirty acres of slightly rolling terrain dotted with many stately shade trees.

WILLIAM G. STRATTON STATE PARK—
Located in Morris, it provides public boat access to the Illinois River. Picnicking and fishing are popular here.

83

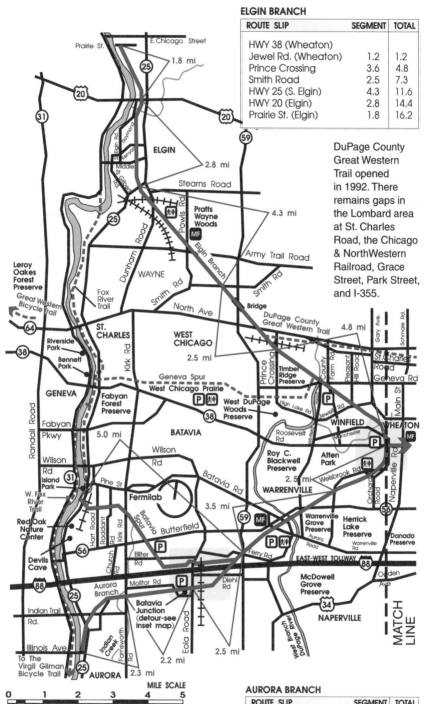

ELGIN BRANCH

ROUTE SLIP	SEGMENT	TOTAL
HWY 38 (Wheaton)		
Jewel Rd. (Wheaton)	1.2	1.2
Prince Crossing	3.6	4.8
Smith Road	2.5	7.3
HWY 25 (S. Elgin)	4.3	11.6
HWY 20 (Elgin)	2.8	14.4
Prairie St. (Elgin)	1.8	16.2

DuPage County Great Western Trail opened in 1992. There remains gaps in the Lombard area at St. Charles Road, the Chicago & NorthWestern Railroad, Grace Street, Park Street, and I-355.

The trail crosses numerous residential streets at grade and several four-lane arterials. There are bridges over the DuPage River (both east & west branch), Klein Creek and a small tributary.

AURORA BRANCH

ROUTE SLIP	SEGMENT	TOTAL
HWY 38 (Wheaton)		
Weisbrook Road	2.5	2.5
Ferry Rd. & HWY 59	3.5	6.0
Eola Rd.	2.5	8.5
Farnsworth Rd. (Aurora)	2.2	10.7
Illinois Ave. (Aurora)	2.3	13.0

Illinois Prairie Path
Batavia and Geneva Spurs
Great Western Trail-DuPage County

Trail Length	Illinois Prairie Path	44.2 miles
	Batavia Spur	5.0 miles
	Geneva Spur	5.0 miles
	Great Western Trail	11.4 miles

Surface	Limestone screenings (Batavia Spur is partially paved)
Location & Setting	Refer to route slips for location of trails. Prairie, wetlands, open spaces, woods, urban communities.
Information	The Illinois Prairie Path (630) 665-5310
County	Cook, DuPage, Kane

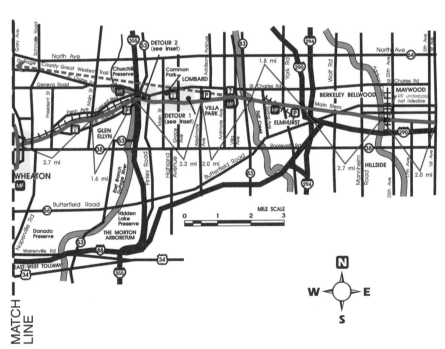

Along much of The Illinois Prairie Path, nature is abundant. Pheasants, flickers, robins, cardinals, chickadees and goldfinch can be found. Many different species of plants are found throughout the seasons. During spring look for mayapples, which look like small green umbrellas popping out of the ground. In summer, violets and onions are in bloom. Autumn brings out goldenrod and asters.

THE ILLINOIS PRAIRIE PATH MAIN STEM

ROUTE SLIP	SEGMENT	TOTAL
HWY 38 (Wheaton)		
Main St. (Glen Ellyn)	2.7	2.7
Du Page River (E. Branch)	1.6	4.3
Westmore Ave. (Lombard)	2.2	6.5
Salt Creek	2.0	8.5
HWY 290 (Elmhurst)	1.8	10.3
Addison Creek	2.7	13.0
First Ave. (Maywood)	2.0	15.0

Illinois Beach State Park

Trail Length	8 miles
Surface	Limestone screenings, packed earth
Location & Setting	Parallels the Lake Michigan shoreline from south of Zion to the Wisconsin State line. Separating the Northern and Southern Units is Commonwealth Edison's power plant. The Northern unit includes the North Point Marina. Additional trail development is planned.

Northern Unit—The path runs from the Marina to San Pond and to the railroad tracks near 7th St. in Winthrop Harbor.
Southern Unit —The path extends along 29th Street to connect to the Zion Bikeway. |
| **Information** | Zion Beach State Park (847) 662-4811 |
| **County** | Lake |

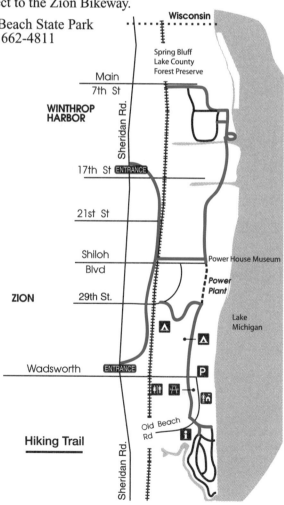

FACILITIES

- 🅰 Camping
- ? Info
- P Parking
- 🎋 Picnic
- 🚻 Restrooms
- 🏠 Shelter
- 🚰 Water
- **MF** Multi Facilities Available

Refreshments	First Aid
Telephone	Picnic
Restrooms	Lodging

Hiking Trail

Independence Grove

Trail Length	7 miles
Surface	Paved, crushed limestone
Location & Setting	A 7 mile trail system located off Rte 137 in north Libertyville. There is both a paved and a crushed stone trail overlooking and circling a 115 acre lake. Facilities include bicycle & boat rental, water, restrooms, picnic area and a Visitors Center. Opened in 2001.
Information	Lake County Forest Preserve (847) 367-6640
County	Lake

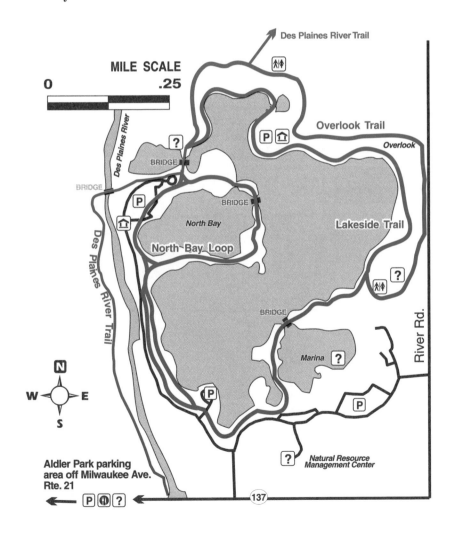

Des Plaines River Trail

MILE SCALE

0   .25

Des Plaines River

BRIDGE

BRIDGE

Des Plaines River Trail

Overlook Trail

Overlook

North Bay

North Bay Loop

Lakeside Trail

BRIDGE

Marina

River Rd.

N
W   E
S

BRIDGE

Natural Resource
Management Center

Aldler Park parking
area off Milwaukee Ave.
Rte. 21

137

Indian Boundry Division

Trail Length	10 .8 miles
Surface	Natural groomed
Uses	Fat tire bicycling, hiking, horseback riding
Location & Setting	Located along the east bank of the Des Plaines River in northwest Cook County. The trail begins at Madison Street, east of First Avenue in Maywood, and follows the Des Plaines River north to Touhy Avenue, east of the Tri-State Tollway in Des Plaines.
Information	Emergency Assistance 911 Cook County Forest Preserve District (708) 366-9420
County	Cook

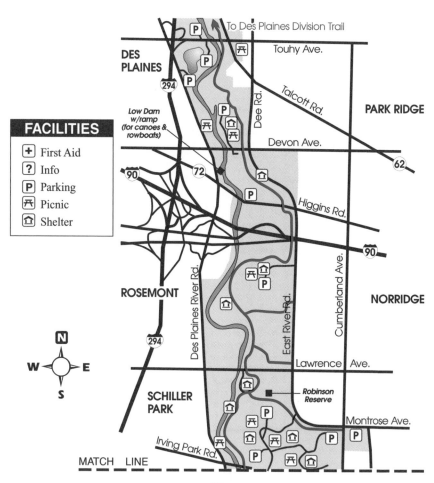

Bicycling Trail
Alternate Use Trail
Roadway

The trail connects to the Salt Creek Forest Preserve to the south and to the Des Plaines River Division to the north.

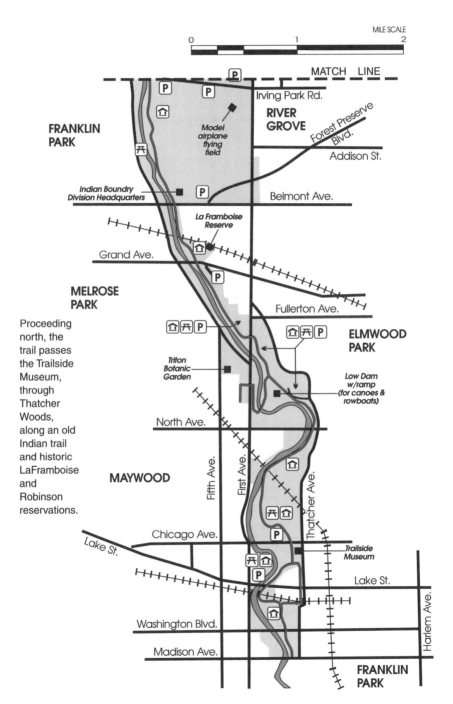

MILE SCALE

0   1   2

MATCH LINE

Irving Park Rd.

RIVER GROVE

FRANKLIN PARK

Model airplane flying field

Forest Preserve Blvd.

Addison St.

Indian Boundry Division Headquarters

Belmont Ave.

La Framboise Reserve

Grand Ave.

MELROSE PARK

Fullerton Ave.

Proceeding north, the trail passes the Trailside Museum, through Thatcher Woods, along an old Indian trail and historic LaFramboise and Robinson reservations.

ELMWOOD PARK

Triton Botanic Garden

Low Dam w/ramp (for canoes & rowboats)

North Ave.

MAYWOOD

Fifth Ave.

First Ave.

Thatcher Ave.

Chicago Ave.

Lake St.

Trailside Museum

Lake St.

Washington Blvd.

Harlem Ave.

Madison Ave.

FRANKLIN PARK

Jane Addams Trail

Trail Length   14.5 miles (20 miles when extended to WI state line)

Surface   Crushed stone

Location & Setting   This 17 mile trail runs along Richland Creek between the city of Freeport and the Wisconsin State line. It will eventually be extended to Madison. The southern terminus connects to the Grand Illinois Trail. Setting is rolling hills, open fields and farmland.

Information   Freeport Economic Foundation   (815) 756-1350

County   Stephenson

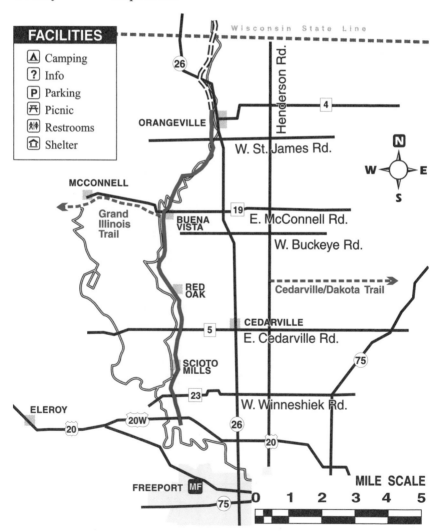

Jubilee College State Park

Trail Length	15 miles
Surface	Natural – groomed
Location & Setting	Jubilee College State Park is located about 10 miles northwest of Peoria between the towns of Kickapoo and Brimfield. The Park offers some 15 miles of mountain bike trails, and is open to horseback riding and snowmobiling. Setting is rolling terrain and open prairie.
Information	Jubilee College State Park (309) 446-3758
County	Peoria

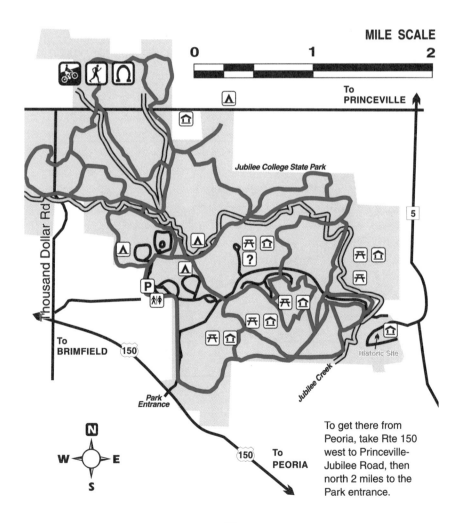

MILE SCALE

To PRINCEVILLE

Jubilee College State Park

5

Thousand Dollar Rd

To BRIMFIELD 150

?

Historic Site

Jubilee Creek

Park Entrance

To PEORIA 150

N
W E
S

To get there from Peoria, take Rte 150 west to Princeville-Jubilee Road, then north 2 miles to the Park entrance.

Jim Edgar Panther Creek Wildlife Area

Trail Length & Surface	9 miles paved & 17 miles groomed for mountain biking
Location & Setting	Within the Jim Edgar Panther Creek WC is a 9 mile paved trail, a 17 mile mountain bike and hiking trail and 26 miles of hiking/equestrian trails. The Wildlife Area is located between Chandlerville and Virginia, east of the Illinois River and north of Jacksonville. The setting is Panther Creek, a 210 acre lake and its tributaries, and surrounding fields of native grass and wild flowers. The main access to the paved trail is parking lot O-11. The mountain bike trailhead is at the west lake day use area just south of Gates Road. The mountain bike trail is closed between November 1 and April 15, but remains open to hikers.
Information	Jim Edgar Panther Creek Wildlife Area (217)452-7741
County	Cass

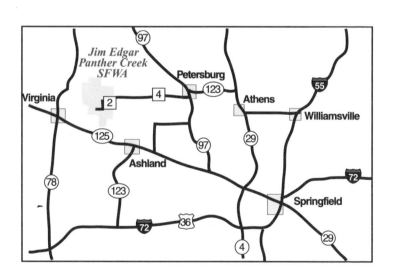

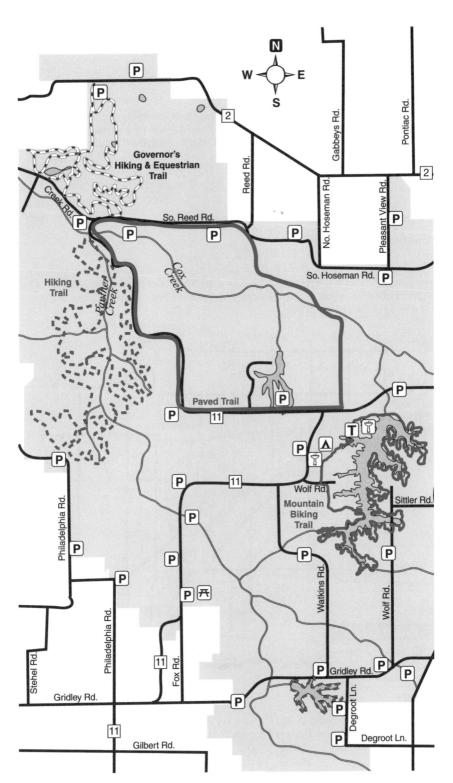

Kankakee River State Park

Trail Length	8 miles
Surface	Crushed limestone
Location & Setting	Located about 8 miles northwest of Kankakee in northeast Illinois. The park consists of some 4,000 acres with Routes 102 on the north and 113 on the south. Both I-55 and I-57 provide convenient accesses. Straddles the Kankakee River - bluffs, canyons, heavy woods. Effort level ranges from easy to difficult.
Information	Kankakee River State Park (815) 933-1383
County	Will

The bicycle trails begins at Davis Creek Area and travels to the Chippewa Campground. At one point it crosses a suspension bridge. There are 12 miles of cross country ski trails, and a 3 mile hiking trail with views of limestone canyons and a frothy waterfall. There is also a 12 mile equestrian trail.

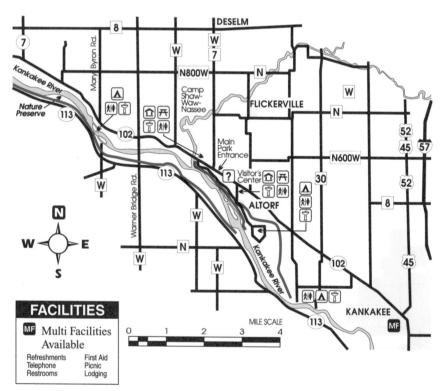

FACILITIES

MF Multi Facilities Available

Refreshments	First Aid
Telephone	Picnic
Restrooms	Lodging

MILE SCALE

0   1   2   3   4

Canoe rentals are available at Bird Park in Kankakee (815)932-6555. It's a four to six hour trip to the park from there. There is a concession stand, camping and picnicking areas. Bicycle rentals are available (815)932-3337.

Kickapoo State Park

Trail Length	11.5 miles (loops)
Surface	Natural, groomed, single track
Location & Setting	Located in east central Illinois, 10 miles west of Indiana and 35 miles east of Champaign/Urbana. Kickapoo State Park consists of 2,842 acres and has 22 deep water ponds. The setting is made up of lushly forested uplands and bottomlands along the Middle Fork of the Vermilion River. There is easy access from I-74 and connecting roads surrounding the park.
Information	Kickapoo State Park (217) 442-4915
County	Vermilion

Kickapoo owes its crystal clear pond and forested ridges to the regenerative powers of nature, which reclaimed the area over the past 50 years after a century of strip mining.

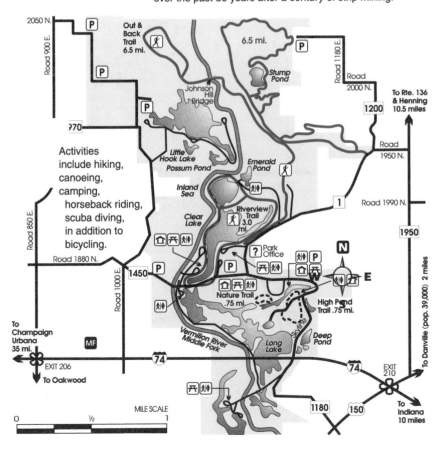

Kishwaukee Kiwanis Pathway

Trail Length	6.5 miles
Surface	Paved
Location & Setting	The Kishwaukee Kiwanis Pathway is located in DeKalb and runs along the Kishwaukee River Between Lions Park and Hopkins Park. The setting is riverfront and open space.
Information	DeKalb Park District (815) 756-9939
County	DeKalb

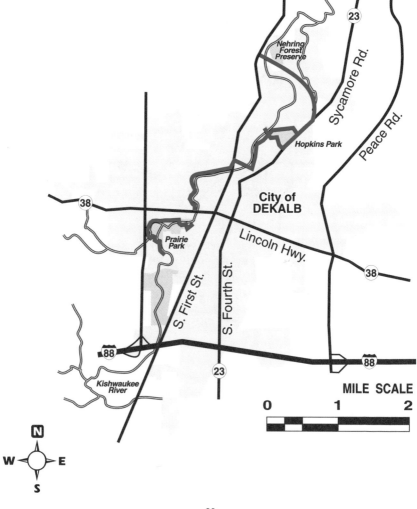

Kiwanis Trail

Trail Length	6.5 miles
Surface	Paved (10 feet), connecting low speed streets
Location & Setting	Located on the north side of the Rock River in Moline. It extends from 7th Street to 60th.
Information	Moline Park and Recreation Department (309) 797-0785
County	Rock Island

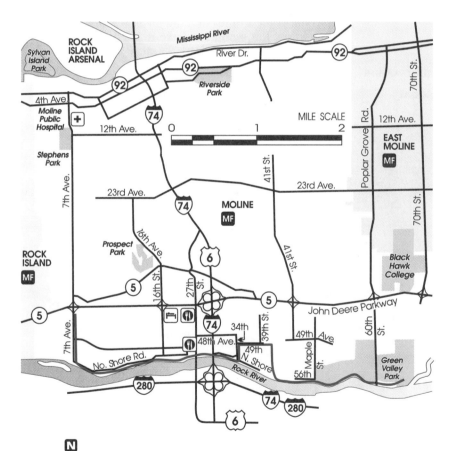

The trail is open from sunrise to sunset, year round. Food, lodging, sight-seeing facilities are readily available.

Lake Le-Aqua-Na State Park

Trail Length	7 miles
Surface	Limestone screenings, dirt.
Location & Setting	This is a beautiful 715 acre state park with a 40 acre lake and large tracts of oak, history, walnut, and pine trees. It's located near Freeport in northwest Illinois. The landscape is rolling. In addition to these trails, facilities include a small swimming beach, picnic areas, shelters and camping. The camp store is open from Memorial Day through Labor Day.
	From Freeport, take Rte 20 west to IL 73 north. Take IL73 north for 2 miles into the town of Lena. Left on Lena Street for .4 miles to Lake Road, then right (north) for about 3 miles to the Park entrance.
Information	Lake Le-Aqua-Na State Park (815)369-4282
County	Stephenson

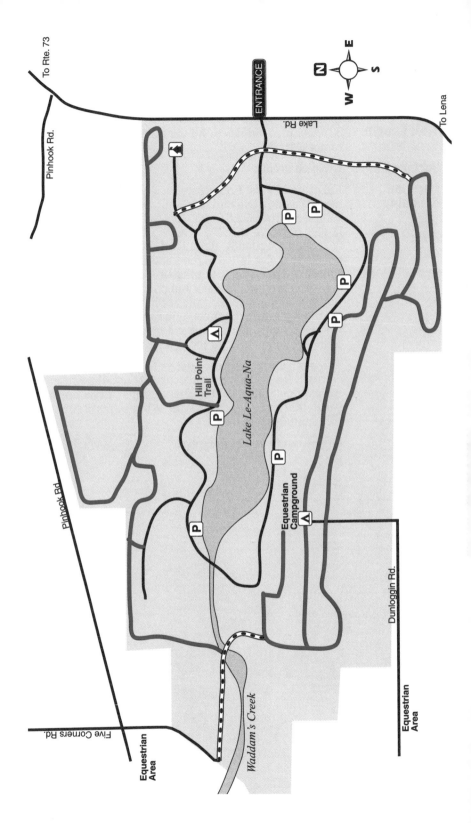

Lakewood Forest Preserve Millennium Trail

Trail Length	3 miles (plus 9 miles of hiking trails & 6.5 miles of horse trails)
Surface	Crushed granite
Location & Setting	Lakewood Forest Preserve is located near Wauconda, west of Mundelein and north of Lake Zurich, in southwestern Lake County. It is the Lake County's largest preserve with 2,578 acres of rolling hills, dense oak woods, wetlands, fields, and several lakes and ponds. It is also home to the Lake County Discovery Museum. Hikers have 9 miles of looped trail that wind their way around the lakes and ponds and through the forest. There is also 6.5 miles of horse trails. The trails are mostly crushed granite, wide, and generally flat. Biking is only allowed on the 3 mile Lakewood section of the Millennium Trail located east of Fairfield Road.
	The main entrance is on Route 176, just west of Fairfield Road. This entrance takes you to the Museum. Another entrance is at the intersections of Ivanhoe and Fairfield Roads. Go east for the Winter Sports Area and Millennium Trail.
Information	Lake County Forest Preserves (847) 367-6640
County	Lake

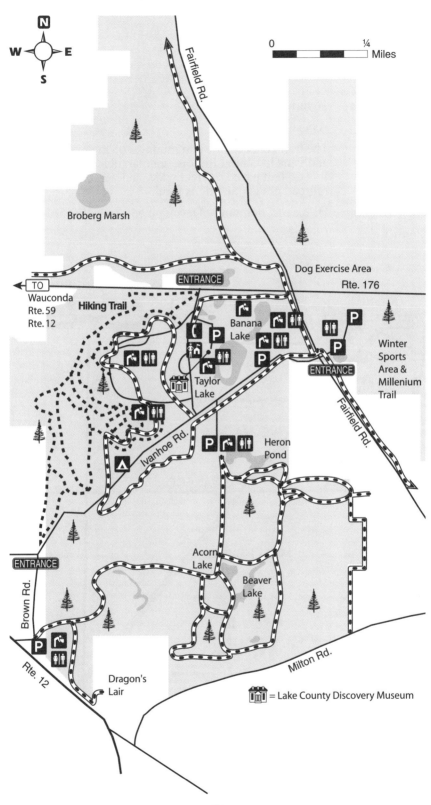

N
W · E
S

Fairfield Rd.

0 ¼
Miles

Broberg Marsh

TO
Wauconda
Rte. 59
Rte. 12

Hiking Trail

Dog Exercise Area
ENTRANCE
Rte. 176

Banana
Lake

ENTRANCE

Winter
Sports
Area &
Millenium
Trail

Taylor
Lake

Ivanhoe Rd.

Heron
Pond

Fairfield Rd.

Acorn
Lake

Beaver
Lake

ENTRANCE

Brown Rd.

Rte. 12

Dragon's
Lair

Milton Rd.

= Lake County Discovery Museum

101

Lincoln Prairie Trail

8-27-05
Rode this —

Trail Length	16 miles
Surface	Asphalt
Location & Setting	The trail connects the communities of Taylorville and Pana in central Illinois, and parallels Hwy 29. It is asphalt paved, 10-feet wide, and was built on old railroad grade. Setting is rural.
Information	Office of Community Development (217) 562-3109
County	Christian

Not impressed w/ amenities

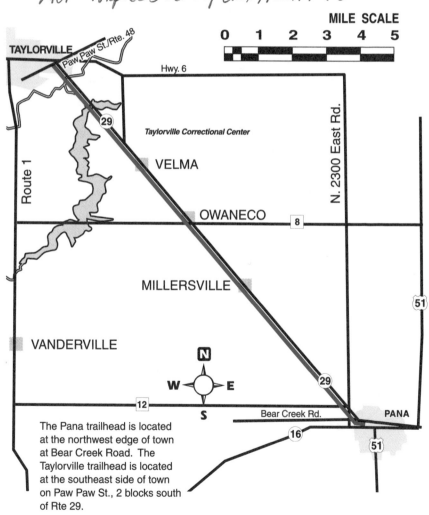

MILE SCALE

0 1 2 3 4 5

TAYLORVILLE
Paw Paw St./Rte. 48
Hwy. 6

(29)

Taylorville Correctional Center

VELMA

Route 1

N. 2300 East Rd.

OWANECO 8

MILLERSVILLE

(51)

VANDERVILLE

N

W — E

S

(29)

12

Bear Creek Rd. **PANA**

16

(51)

The Pana trailhead is located at the northwest edge of town at Bear Creek Road. The Taylorville trailhead is located at the southeast side of town on Paw Paw St., 2 blocks south of Rte 29.

Lost Bridge Trail

Trail Length	5 miles
Surface	Paved
Location & Setting	The Lost Bridge Trail, stretching from Springfield's east side to the town of Rochester, is built on an old railroad right-of-way. There is a connecting trail to Rochester Community Park, with access to parking, water and restrooms. Dense trees line each side of the trail and shields bicyclists from nearby traffic noises.
Information	Village of Rochester (217) 498-7192
County	Sangamon

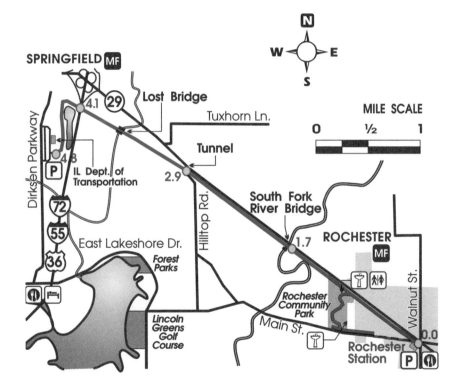

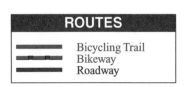

Long Prairie Trail

Trail Length	14.2 miles
Surface	Asphalt
Location & Setting	The east trailhead is on County Line Road about a half mile north of Hwy. 173. The entrance is on the left and there is ample parking. The west trailhead is at Argyle Road, at the Winnebago County line. Open areas, farmland, small communities.
Information	Boone County Conservation District (815) 547-7935
County	Boone

There are plans to extend the
trail 3.3 miles east to an area
near the city of Harvard.

MILE SCALE

0   1   2   3

FACILITIES

✚	First Aid
🛏	Lodging
P	Parking
🍴	Refreshments
🚻	Restrooms
MF	Multi Facilities Available

Refreshments	First Aid
Telephone	Picnic
Restrooms	Lodging

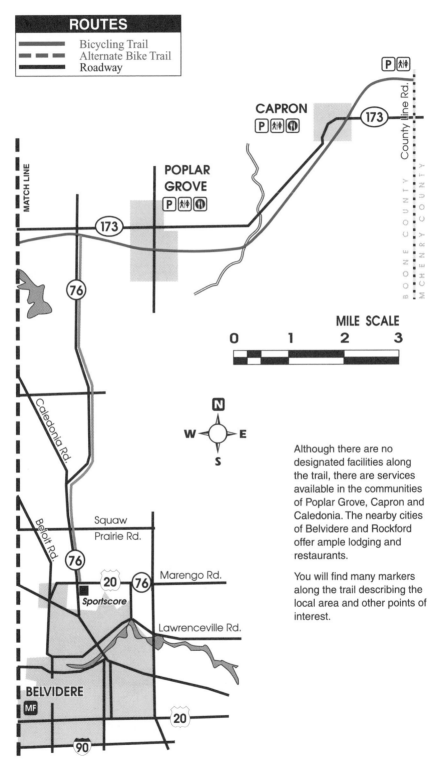

ROUTES

Bicycling Trail
Alternate Bike Trail
Roadway

CAPRON

POPLAR GROVE

173

76

Caledonia Rd.

Squaw Prairie Rd.

20 76 Marengo Rd.

Sportscore

Lawrenceville Rd.

BELVIDERE

MF

20

90

County Line Rd.

BOONE COUNTY

MCHENRY COUNTY

MATCH LINE

MILE SCALE

0   1   2   3

N
W E
S

Although there are no designated facilities along the trail, there are services available in the communities of Poplar Grove, Capron and Caledonia. The nearby cities of Belvidere and Rockford offer ample lodging and restaurants.

You will find many markers along the trail describing the local area and other points of interest.

Loud Thunder Forest Preserve

Trail Length	8 miles
Surface	Natural
Location & Setting	Loud Thunder has 8 miles of bi-directional single track. There are deep woods, with many climbs and downhills. Potable water is available at the horse coral during the summer. Much of the trail is marked and signed. The park closes at 10 pm.
	The park is located 10 miles west of Milan and 5 miles west of Andalusia, off Hwy 92. Take Hwy 92 out of the quad cities until you reach Loud Thunder Road. Take a right turn and follow signs to the horse coral. The trails are off to your left.
Information	Loud Thunder Forest Preserve (309) 795-1040
County	Rock Island

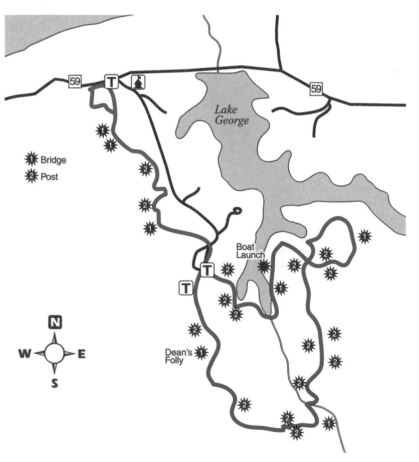

Lowell Parkway

Trail Length	3.5 miles
Surface	Screenings
Location & Setting	Located in the town of Dixon in northwest Illinois. The path is a converted railbed.
Information	Dixon Park District (815) 284-3306
County	Lee

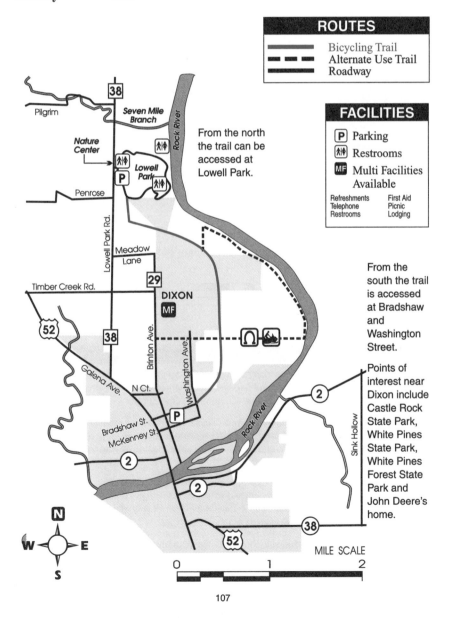

ROUTES

Bicycling Trail
Alternate Use Trail
Roadway

FACILITIES

P   Parking

Restrooms

MF   Multi Facilities Available

Refreshments   First Aid
Telephone   Picnic
Restrooms   Lodging

From the north the trail can be accessed at Lowell Park.

From the south the trail is accessed at Bradshaw and Washington Street.

Points of interest near Dixon include Castle Rock State Park, White Pines State Park, White Pines Forest State Park and John Deere's home.

MILE SCALE

Mattoon to Charleston Trail

Trail Length	12 miles
Surface	Limestone Screenings
Location & Setting	The Mattoon to Charleston Trail is built along a ComEd right-of-way between the two cities. The surface is limestone screenings. The setting is open and farmland, and flat.
Information	Charleston Chamber of Commerce (217) 345-7041
County	Coles

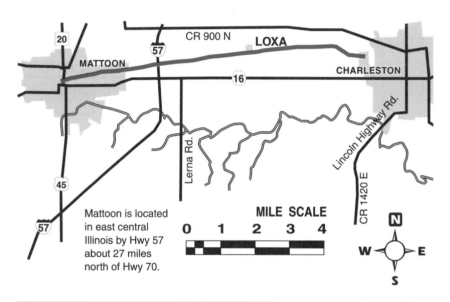

Mattoon is located in east central Illinois by Hwy 57 about 27 miles north of Hwy 70.

Right-of-Way Laws

Right-of-way means that one person has the right to go ahead of another. This applies to bicycle riders, vehicle drivers, and pedestrians. Right-of-way is something to give, not take. If others don't follow the rules, let them have the right-of-way.

At a four-way stop intersection, the driver or bicycle rider who arrives first at the intersection should be the first one to go. After making a complete stop, proceed only when it is safe to do so. Drivers and bicycle riders are expected to take their turns and go one by one through the intersection after they come to a complete stop.

At an unmarked intersection or crossing where there are no traffic signs or signals, the driver or bicycle rider on the left must yield to those on the right. When you drive out of an alley or driveway, you must stop and yield the right-of-way to pedestrians and vehicles before you cross the sidewalk or enter the street.

Emergency vehicles operating with their lights flashing and siren sounding always have the right-of-way. The law requires that you pull over to the side and stop it necessary.

McDonald Woods
Forest Preserve

Trail Length	4.5 miles
Surface	Limestone screenings
Location & Setting	McDonald Woods is a glacial landscape of rolling hills, steep ravines and wetlands, and a great place to hike or ride your bike. You can wander through evergreen forests and meadows nestled in a valley of solitude. There are 4.5 miles of trail, of which 3.5 miles is open to biking. The granite trail loops around two large marsh ponds in a valley. The preserve is open from 6:30 am to sunset. Take Route 45 north to Grass Lake Road, then west for .7 miles to the entrance on the south side of the road.
Information	Lake County Forest Preserves (847) 369-6640
County	Lake

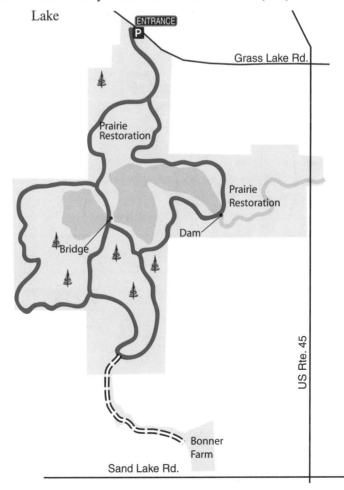

McDowell Grove
Forest Preserve

Trail Length	5.6 miles
Surface	Mowed turf
Location & Setting	This preserve is located in southwest DuPage County on Raymond Road at McDowell Avenue between Ogden Avenue and the East-West Tollway (Hwy. 88) and south of Warrenville.
Information	Forest Preserve District of DuPage County (630) 933-7200
County	DuPage

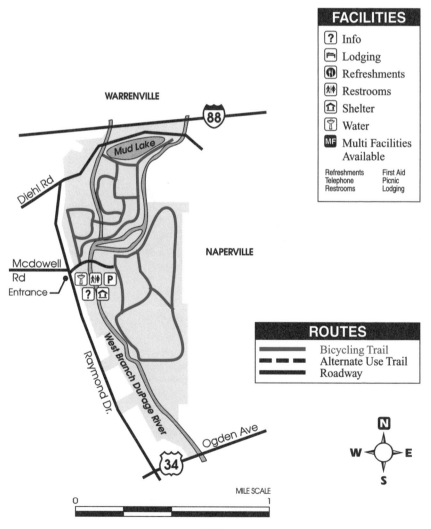

FACILITIES

- [?] Info
- [=] Lodging
- [⊕] Refreshments
- [⋔⋔] Restrooms
- [⌂] Shelter
- [T] Water
- **MF** Multi Facilities Available

Refreshments   First Aid
Telephone   Picnic
Restrooms   Lodging

WARRENVILLE

88

Mud Lake

Diehl Rd

NAPERVILLE

Mcdowell Rd
Entrance

[T][⋔⋔][P]
[?][⌂]

West Branch DuPage River

Raymond Dr.

ROUTES

━━━ Bicycling Trail
─ ─ ─ Alternate Use Trail
━━━ Roadway

Ogden Ave

34

N
W E
S

MILE SCALE

0   1

Middlefork Savanna
Forest Preserve

Trail Length	4.5 miles
Surface, Location & Setting	This 567 acre Preserve is located in southeast Lake County near Lake Forest. There are 4 miles of gravel trails open to hiking, bicycling, and cross-country skiing, plus another half mile of mowed path for hikers. Middlefork is home to a rare tallgrass savanna, and features a mix of oak savanna and woodlands, wet and mesic prairies, meadows and marshes. Open hours are 6:30 a.m. to sunset. The entrance is located near Waukegan Road (Route 43) and Middlefork Drive north of Route 60. Turn west on Middlefork Drive and follow signs to the Preserve parking area.
Information	Lake County Forest Preserves (847) 367-6640
County	Lake

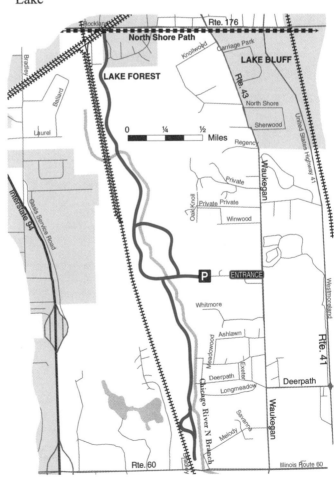

Millenium Trail

Trail Length	35 miles
Surface	Gravel
Location & Setting	This is 35 mile trail under development that will connect the central, western and northern Lake County communities and Forest Preserves. As of this publication the trail 13.5 miles of this trail is now open, from Midlothian Road in Mundelein west through a section of the Lakewood Forest Preserve, and then north to the Singling Hills Forest Preserve.
Information	Lake County Forest Preserves (847) 367-6640
County	Lake

Millennium Trail – Hawley Street

Trail Length   3 miles
Surface   Asphalt

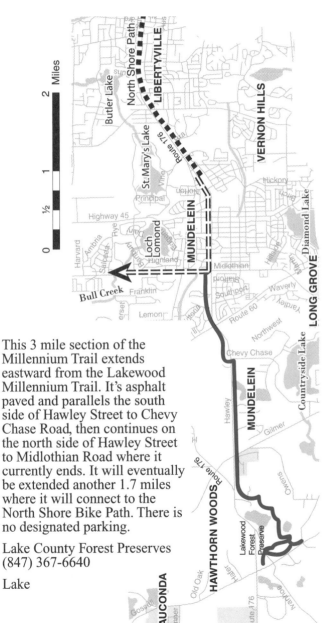

Location & Setting

This 3 mile section of the Millennium Trail extends eastward from the Lakewood Millennium Trail. It's asphalt paved and parallels the south side of Hawley Street to Chevy Chase Road, then continues on the north side of Hawley Street to Midlothian Road where it currently ends. It will eventually be extended another 1.7 miles where it will connect to the North Shore Bike Path. There is no designated parking.

Information

Lake County Forest Preserves
(847) 367-6640

County

Lake

Moraine Hills State Park

Trail Length	11 miles	
Surface	Limestone screenings	
Location & Setting	Located 3 miles south of the city of McHenry, there is an easily recognized sign at the junction of Hwy. 176 and River Road directing you to parking. Wooded, wetlands, and is well groomed with many small hills and curves.	
Information	Moraine Hills State Park	(815) 385-1624
County	McHenry	

Trails are one-way and color coded. There are three loops:
Lake Defiance- 3.72 miles with red markers
Leather Leaf Bog- 3.18 miles with blue markers
Fox River- 2.0 miles with yellow markers

Moraine Hills State Park consists of 1,690 acres. There is trail access at McHenry Dam.

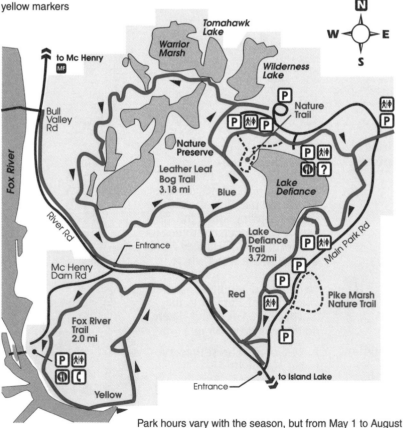

Park hours vary with the season, but from May 1 to August 31, the park is open from 6am to 9pm.

North Shore Path

Trail Length	8.5 miles
Surface	Limestone screenings, paved
Location & Setting	Proceeds west from just south of Rock-land Rd. (Hwy. 176) in Lake Bluff to Hwy. 45 in Mundelein. Surburban, open and lightly wooded areas.
Information	Lake County Dept. of Transportation (847) 362-3950
County	Lake

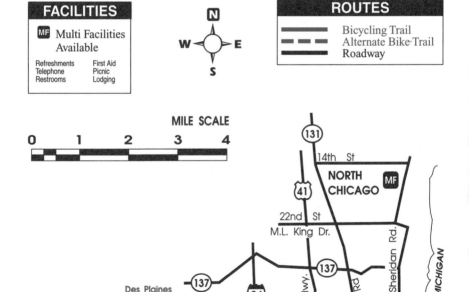

North Branch Bicycle Trail Techny Trail

Trail Length	20 miles (plus bikeways)
Surface	Paved
Location & Setting	Open spaces, wooded—extends from the Chicago Botanic Gardens south approximately 20 miles to Caldwell and Devon Avenues in Chicago.
Information	Forest Preserve District of Cook County (708) 366-9420
County	Cook

POINTS OF INTEREST

- Ⓐ Chicago Botanic Garden
- Ⓑ Skokie Lagoons
- Ⓒ Blue Star Memorial Woods
- Ⓓ Glenview Woods
- Ⓔ Harms Woods
- Ⓕ Chick Evans Golf Course
- Ⓖ Linne Woods
- Ⓗ Miami Woods
- Ⓘ Clayton Smith Woods
- Ⓙ Whealan Pool
- Ⓚ Edgebrook Golf Course
- Ⓛ Billy Caldwell Golf Course

MILE SCALE
0   1   2   3

ROUTES

- ━━━ Bicycling Trail
- ━■━■ Bikeway
- ━ ━ ━ Alternate Bike Trail
- ═ ═ ═ Planned Trail
- ━━━ Roadway

FACILITIES

- [?] Info
- **MF** Multi Facilities Available

Refreshments	First Aid
Telephone	Picnic
Restrooms	Lodging

EMERGENCY ASSISTANCE

Forest Preserve Police at
708/366-8210 or
708/366-8211

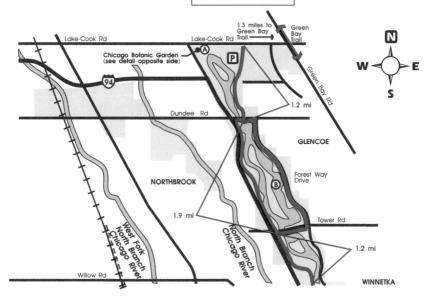

The trail winds along the North Branch of the Chicago River and the Skokie Lagoons, providing access to various picnic groves and communities in addition to the Botanic Gardens.

MILE SCALE

0   1   2   3

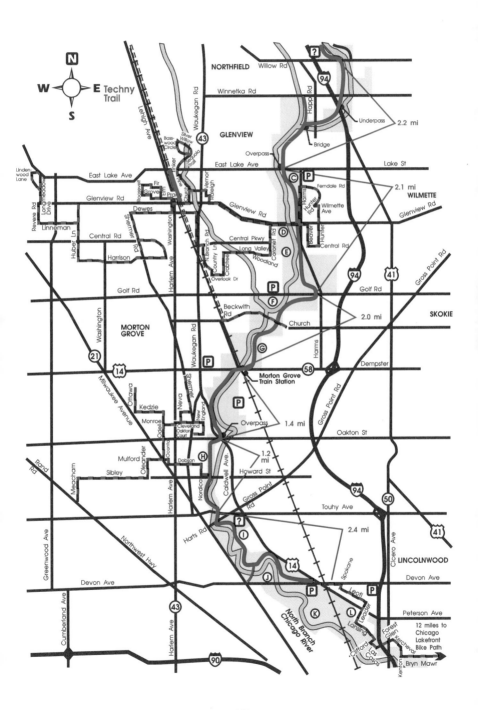

Old Plank Road Trail

Trail Length	21 miles
Surface	Asphalt
Location & Setting	Located in Cook and Will Counties, the trail the trail will become a major link in the Grand Illinois Trail. It extends from Western Avenue in Park Forest to Cherry Hill Road east of Joliet. Plans include its extension to the I & M Canal State Trail. Hickory Creek Junction, a half mile north of the trail, serves as an access point with parking and a pedestrian bridge over Highway 30. The setting is urban with open and some wooded areas.
Information	Will County Forest Preserve (815) 727-8700
County	Cook, Will

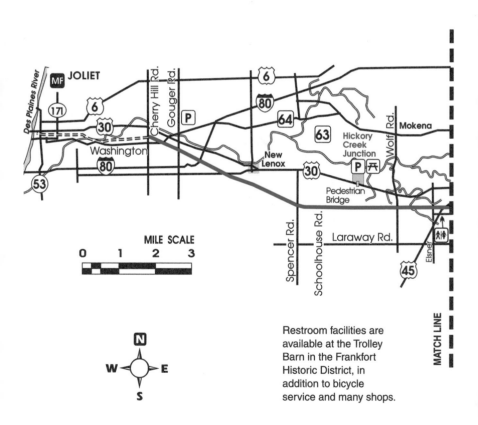

MILE SCALE

0   1   2   3

N
W ◄─◊─► E
S

Restroom facilities are available at the Trolley Barn in the Frankfort Historic District, in addition to bicycle service and many shops.

FACILITIES

🔧 Bike Repair

Ⓟ Parking

🛐 Picnic

🚹🚺 Restrooms

🚰 Water

MF Multi Facilities
Available

Refreshments	First Aid
Telephone	Picnic
Restrooms	Lodging

ROUTES

━━━ Bicycling Trail
═ ═ ═ Planned Trail
━━━ Roadway

RULES OF THE TRAIL

Hours of operation are from dawn to dusk

No alcoholic beverages

No motorized vehicles

No camping or fires

Stay on the trail

Picking or damaging plants on the trail is prohibited

Obey all posted signs

The METRA station, located between Park Forest and Matteson, provides transportation to the Chicago Loop. There is parking, bike racks and lockers at the Park Forest municipal parking lot.

From the eastern trailhead, the Sauk Trail Woods is located a half mile to the east. Plans are to acquire a railroad right-of-way in Chicago Heights to connect these trails.

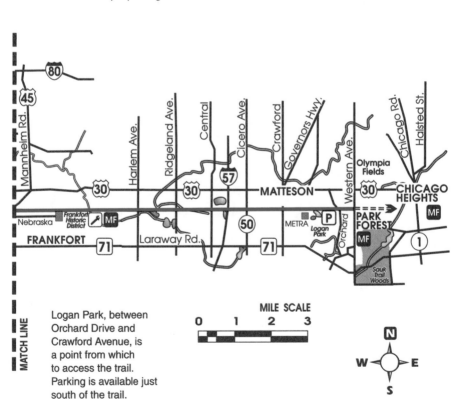

Logan Park, between Orchard Drive and Crawford Avenue, is a point from which to access the trail. Parking is available just south of the trail.

MILE SCALE

0   1   2   3

Oak Brook Bike Paths

Trail Length	17 miles (approximately) and some 5+ miles of designated bikeways
Surface	Paved, screenings
Location & Setting	Oak Brook is located in east central DuPage County. The bike paths and bikeways are located throughout Oak Brook. There are multiple accesses to the paths as is parking. The setting is urban, open and wooded.
Information	Oak Brook Park District (630) 990-4233 1300 Forest Gate Road Oak Brook, IL 60521
County	DuPage

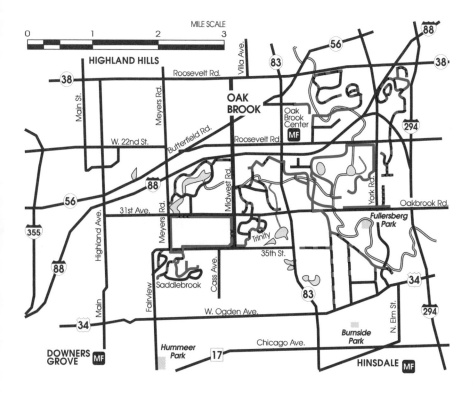

The paths are well marked with signs, and several of the major roads provide tunnels for safe passage across.

Oakhurst Forest Preserve

Trail Length	5 miles
Surface	Paved and gravel
Location & Setting	The 5 mile Patterson Lake Trail is located in the Oakhurst Forest Preserve. Trail surface is paved and gravel. The Preserve contains a 55 acre lake/marsh complex with excellent opportunities for wildlife observation. The setting is woods, open areas and wetlands.
	Oakhurst Forest Preserve is off 5th Avenue, approximately ½ mile east of Farnsworth Avenue in Aurora.
Information	Kane County Forest Preserves (630) 232-5980
County	Kane

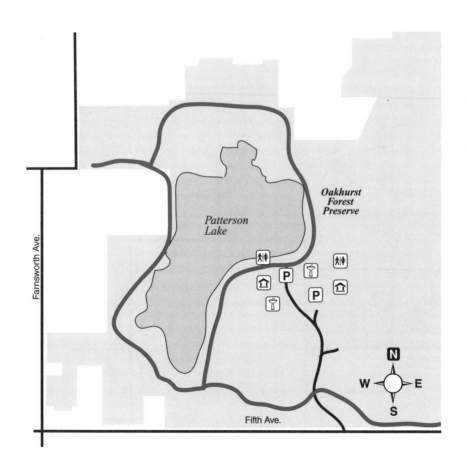

Palos & Sag Valley Forest Preserve- I & M Canal Trail

Trail Length	Palos is 30.0 miles, I & M Canal is 8.9 miles
Surface	Palos is Natural & groomed, I & M Canal is paved
Location & Setting	Palos located in southwest Cook County, mostly hilly and forested with many upland meadows, lakes ponds and sloughs. I & M Canal open and flat.
Information	Palos Forest Preserve (708) 361-1536
County	Cook

ROUTES

——————— Bicycling Trail
– – – – – Alternate Use Trail
——————— Roadway

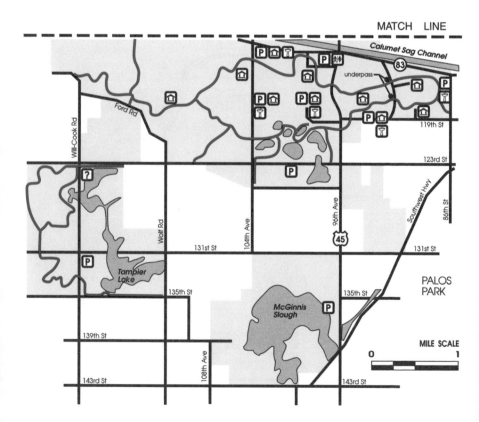

A suggested trail access is by 104th St. (Willow Springs Avenue) and Hwy. 171 (Archer Ave.)

There is a parking lot with the paved trail running through it. Nearby is a visitors center that explains the history of the National Heritage Corridor.

The woodlands provide colorful autumn foliage as well as an abundance of wildlife.

N W E S

MILE SCALE
0 — 1

WILLOW SPRINGS

Wolf Rd

Willow Springs Rd

German Church Rd

County Line Rd

I&M CANAL BICYCLE TRAIL

3.3 mi loop

79th St

Wentworth

171

45

To HICKORY HILLS

87th

Columbia Woods

91st St

2.3 mi

Illinois and Michigan Canal

87th St

104th Ave

MULTI-USE TRAIL

95th St

To PALOS HILLS

Des Plaines River

Sanitary Drainage and Ship Canal

Archer Ave

3.3 mi loop

171

107th St

D C

83

Saganashkee Slough

Calumet Sag Channel

83

45

B

A

?

45

107th St

PALOS & SAG VALLEY FOREST PRESERVE

MATCH LINE

Bicycle Maintenance Checklist

Inspect your bicycle for the following:

Wheels are securely attached, properly adjusted and spin freely with all spokes in place.

All reflectors are clean and intact.

The seat and handlebars are adjusted to a comfortable position with all nuts and bolts tightened.

Hand grips are secure.

Caliper brake pads are not worn and are properly adjusted.

FACILITIES

?	Info
P	Parking
舟	Picnic
⌂	Shelter
🚰	Water
MF	Multi Facilities Available

Refreshments	First Aid
Telephone	Picnic
Restrooms	Lodging

Palatine Trails & Bikeways

Trail Length	15 miles (includes connecting bike routes)
Surface	Paved
Location & Setting	Palatine is located in northwest Cook County. Wooded areas, open spaces, connecting street bikeways, urban.
Information	Palatine Park District (847) 991-0333
County	Cook

ROUTES

Bicycling Trail
Bikeway
Alternate Bike Trail
Roadway

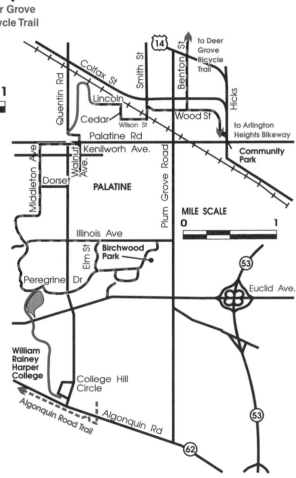

Deer Grove
Bicycle Trail

MILE SCALE (approx.)
0   1

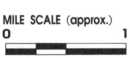

FACILITIES

MF Multi Facilities Available

Refreshments   First Aid
Telephone   Picnic
Restrooms   Lodging

The Palatine Trail extends throughout the Palatine Park district. Combining paved trail with designated side streets, Palatine Trail provides access to schools, Harper College, neighborhood parks, Palatine Hills Golf Course, and other points of interest.

Peace Road Trail

Trail Length	10 miles
Surface	Screenings
Location & Setting	The Peace Road Trail extends from Bethany Road in Sycamore to Pleasant Street in DeKalb. Current access to the Great Western Trail is by way of Airport Road. The setting is rural with farmland, woods and open areas.
Information	DeKalb County Forest Preserve Commission (815) 895-7191
County	DeKalb

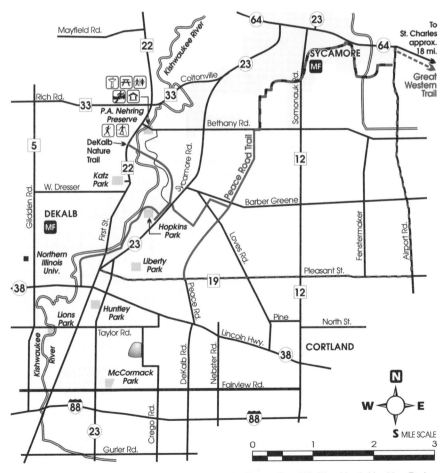

Planned construction includes a path between the Peace Road Trail and both Hopkins Park and the DeKalb Nature Trail. Also planned is an alternate route connecting to the Great Western Trail.

Pecatonica Prairie Path

Trail Length	18 miles
Surface	Ballast
Location & Setting	The trail follows an old railroad right-of-way through Stephenson and Winnebago counties. The eastern trailhead is off Meridian Road just south of Hwy. 20 and west of the city of Rockford. The western trailhead is south of the intersection of Hillcrest Road and River Road, off Hwy. 75, 3 miles east of Freeport. The trails pass through open areas and farmland. Lightly wooded.
Information	Rockford Park District (815) 987-8800
County	Winnebago, Stephenson

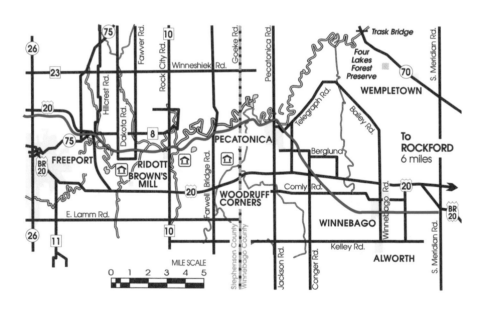

A variety of animals, birds and native wild flowers can be found along the corridor. The right-of-way is owned by Commonwealth Edison, which leases it to Pecatonica Prairie Path, Inc.

FACILITIES

- 🎪 Picnic
- 🚻 Restrooms
- 🏠 Shelter
- 🚰 Water
- **MF** Multi Facilities Available

Refreshments   First Aid
Telephone   Picnic
Restrooms   Lodging

ROUTES

Bicycling Trail
Bikeway
Alternate Bike Trail
Alternate Use Trail
Roadway

Pimiteoui Trail

Trail Length	Approximately 5 miles
Surface	Paved
Location & Setting	Located in the city of Peoria, south to north, from the Robert Mitchell Bridge to the Pioneer Parkway. Urban and open areas.
Information	Peoria Park District (309) 682-1200
County	Peoria

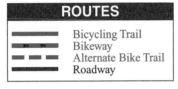

ROUTES

Bicycling Trail
Bikeway
Alternate Bike Trail
Roadway

ROUTE SLIP

Foot of Robert Michel Bridge along waterfront to Woodruff Park.

Cross Adams St., and then head east 75 feet to Abington St.

Follow Abington to Perry Ave., in front of Woodruff High School.

Turn north on Perry, through Springdale Cemetery and under Route 150 to Harvard Ave.

Continue on Harvard Ave., north to Lake Ave., then turn right on Prospect Rd.

Follow Prospect Rd. north for 9 blocks to Kingman Ave., and then turn left on Kingman Ave., following it west to Montclair Ave.

Turn right on Montclair and follow it north to Humbolt Ave., and then to Prospect by Junction City.

Continue along the eastern edge of the railway to Pioneer Parkway.

MILE SCALE

0   1   2   3

Poplar Creek
Forest Preserve

Trail Length	9.5 miles
Surface	Paved
Location & Setting	The 4,500 acre Poplar Creek Forest Preserve is located in northwest Cook County, bordered by Hoffman Estates to the east, west and south, and South Barrington to the north. Wooded, with access to toilets, water and picnic facilities. Portions of the Preserve have been restored to original Illinois prairie. The entrance is on the west side of Barrington Road, south of W. Higgins Road and the Northwest Tollway.
Information	Cook County Forest Preserve District (708) 366-9420
County	Cook

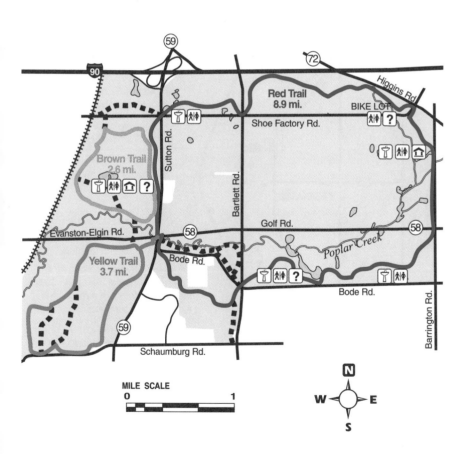

Potawatomi Trail

Trail Length	7 miles
Surface	Natural – groomed
Location & Setting	The Powawatomi Trail is located in Pekin at McNaughton Park. The trail begins and ends at the Totem Pole, behind the stables, and is also open to hiking and horseback riding. Red markers indicate the main trail. The park covers some 700-acres of beautiful woodland and meadows.
Information	Pekin Park District Recreation Department (309) 347-7275
County	Tazewell

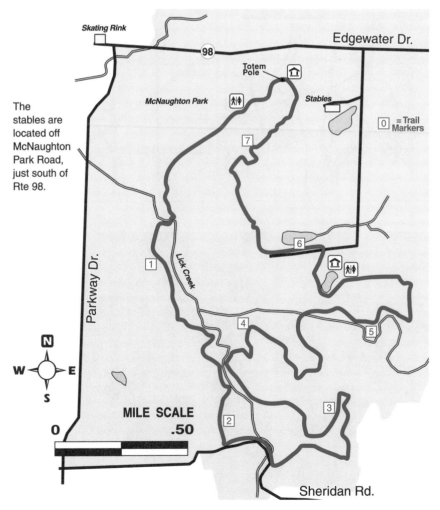

The stables are located off McNaughton Park Road, just south of Rte 98.

Skating Rink

Edgewater Dr.

98

Totem Pole

McNaughton Park

Stables

0 = Trail Markers

7

6

Parkway Dr.

Lick Creek

1

4

5

N
W E
S

MILE SCALE
.50

0

2

3

Sheridan Rd.

Prairie Trail

Trail Length   30 miles

Surface   Paved from Algonquin to Ringwood, ballast & gravel from Ringwood to the Wisconsin border

Location & Setting   From Algonquin north to the Wisconsin State Line. Open space, wooded areas, small communities.

Information   McHenry County Conservation District (815) 338-6223

County   McHenry

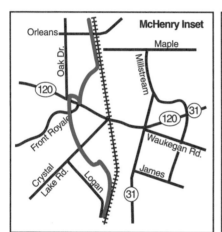

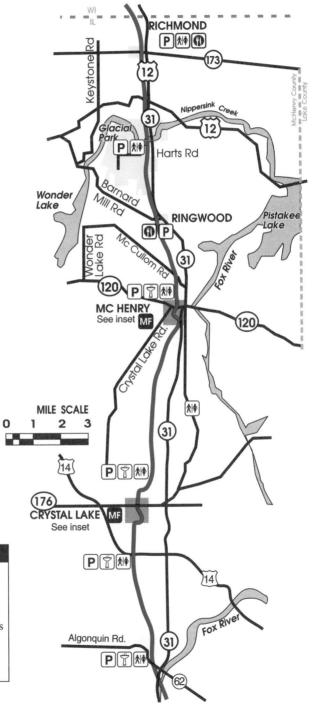

Pratts Wayne Woods Forest Preserve

Trail Length	8.7 miles
Surface	Asphalt, limestone screenings, mowed turf
Location & Setting	Located in the northwest corner of DuPage County between Wayne and Barlett. Access from Powis Road a mile north of Army Trail Road or from the Illinois Prairie Path. It's 2,600 acres include savannas, marshes, meadows and prairies. Wildlife and plants abound.
Information	Forest Preserve District of DuPage County (630) 933-7200
County	DuPage

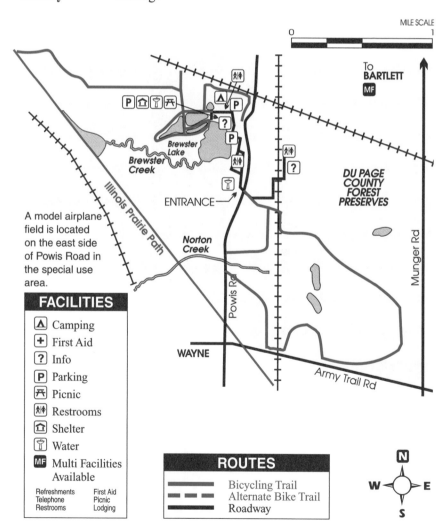

A model airplane field is located on the east side of Powis Road in the special use area.

FACILITIES

- 🅰 Camping
- ➕ First Aid
- ❓ Info
- 🅿 Parking
- 🛆 Picnic
- 🚻 Restrooms
- 🏠 Shelter
- 🥤 Water
- **MF** Multi Facilities Available

Refreshments   First Aid
Telephone   Picnic
Restrooms   Lodging

ROUTES

— Bicycling Trail
--- Alternate Bike Trail
▬ Roadway

MILE SCALE 0 — 1

To BARTLETT

DU PAGE COUNTY FOREST PRESERVES

Brewster Lake
Brewster Creek
ENTRANCE
Norton Creek

Illinois Prairie Path
Powis Rd
Munger Rd
Army Trail Rd
WAYNE

N / W-E / S

Pyramid State Park

Trail Length	16.5 miles
Surface	Natural – groomed
Location & Setting	Pyramid State Park, with 2,528 acres, consists of heavily forested hills with many lakes and ponds. It is located about 5 miles south of Pinckneyville, off Routes 127/13 in southern Illinois. The surface is dirt and generally flat with some hills. Tent and trail camping is available, with both Class C & D campsites. Canoeing is popular.
Information	Pyramid State Park (618) 357-2574
County	Perry

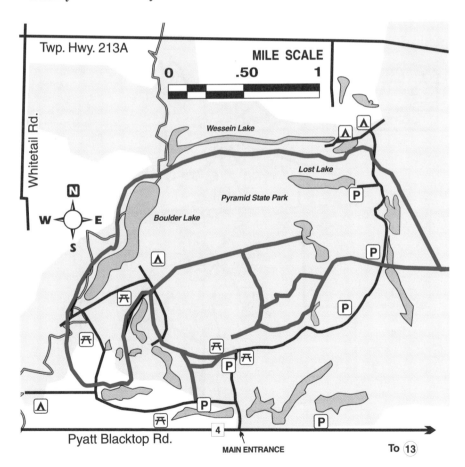

Red Hills State Park

Trail Length	8 miles
Surface	Screenings, natural
Location & Setting	Located in southeastern Illinois between Olney and Lawrence-ville on U.S. Route 50. The park consists of 948 acres with wooded hills, deep ravines, meadows and year round springs.
Information	Red Hills State Park (618) 936-2469
County	Lawrence

Facilities include shaded picnic area with tables and grills, 120 Class A campsites with vehicular access and primitive tent camping. In addition to the bicycling/hiking trail, there is a 5 mile equestrian trail.

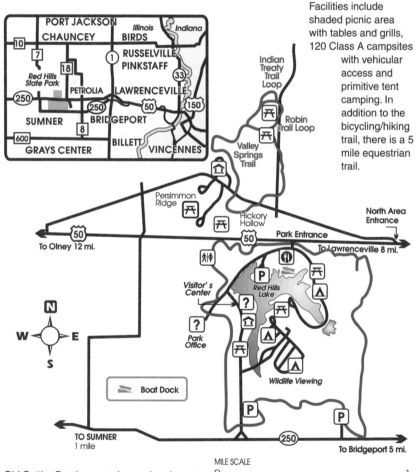

Old Settler Day is a popular weekend event usually scheduled late in April. Red Hill is the highest point of land between St. Louis and Cincinnati. It has a 120 foot tower and cross rising from its summit.

Rend Lake Biking Trails

Trail Length   9.8 miles

Surface   Paved

Location & Setting   The current 9.8 miles of trail are located on the east side of Rend Lake, and consist of the 6-mile trail running through Wayne Fitzgerrlll State Park, and the 3.8 mile Gun Creek Trail that runs from the Visitor Center to the North Marcum Swim Beach. The trails are not connected. Additional trail is under development on the south end of the lake. The trails are paved, and bike rentals are available. Rend Lake is located just north of Benton on Rte 154. There are numerous access points.

Information   Rend Lake Project Office   (618) 742-2493

County   Jefferson, Franklin

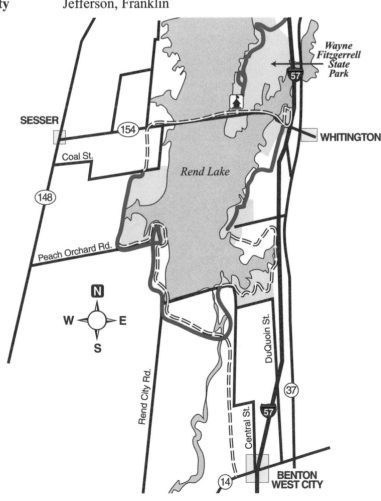

River Trail of Illinois

Trail Length	10.8 miles *just under 1k/ round trip*
Surface	Paved, ~~limestone screenings~~ *round trip*
Location & Setting	Located between Morton and East Peoria. Urban, open and wooded areas, small hills. *large ↙ about 3 mi)*
Information	Fond Du Lac Park District (309) 699-3923
County	Tazewell

rode on 9-3-05

Western Access: Southern end of Robert Michel Bridge across from Steak & Shake Restaurant.

FACILITIES

Ⓐ	Camping
⑦	Info
Ⓟ	Parking
🎪	Picnic
🚻	Restrooms
⛺	Shelter
🚰	Water
MF	Multi Facilities Available

Refreshments	First Aid
Telephone	Picnic
Restrooms	Lodging

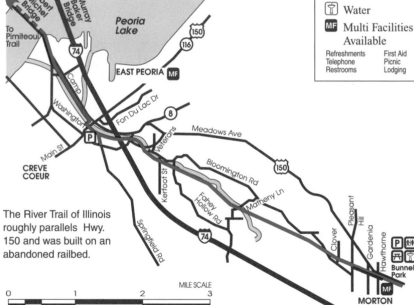

The River Trail of Illinois roughly parallels Hwy. 150 and was built on an abandoned railbed.

Eastern Access: Across from K-Mart and Golden Corral Restaurant.

ROUTES

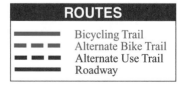

———	Bicycling Trail
– – –	Alternate Bike Trail
▬ ▬ ▬	Alternate Use Trail
▬▬▬	Roadway

N
W—◆—E
S

Explanation of Symbols

TRAIL USES

 Mountain Biking

 Leisure Biking

In Line Skating

Cross-Country Skiing

Hiking

Horseback Riding

Snowmobiling

ROUTES

Multi-Use Trail

Bikeway Trail

Equestrian Trail

Alternate Bike Trail

Alternate Trail

===== Planned Trail

Railroad Tracks

Roadway

FACILITIES

 Bike Repair

A Camping

+ First Aid

? Info

Lodging

P Parking

Picnic

Refreshments

Restrooms

Shelter

Water

MF Multi Facilities
Available

Refreshments   First Aid
Telephone   Picnic
Restrooms   Lodging

ROAD RELATED SYMBOLS

 Interstate Highway

12 U.S. Highway

26 State Highway

K County Highway

AREA DESCRIPTIONS

City, Town

Parks, Preserves

Waterway

 Mileage Scale

Robert McClory Bike Path

Trail Length	25 miles
Surface	Limestone screenings, paved
Uses	Leisure bicycling, cross country skiing, hiking/jogging
Location & Setting	The trail runs north and south from the Cook County line (lake Cook Road) to the Wisconsin border. The setting is surburban, open and lightly wooded areas.
Information	Lake County Dept. of Transportation (847) 362-5950
County	Lake

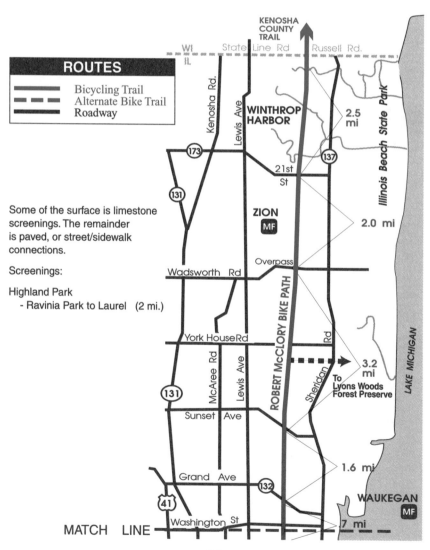

ROUTES

Bicycling Trail
Alternate Bike Trail
Roadway

Some of the surface is limestone screenings. The remainder is paved, or street/sidewalk connections.

Screenings:

Highland Park
- Ravinia Park to Laurel   (2 mi.)

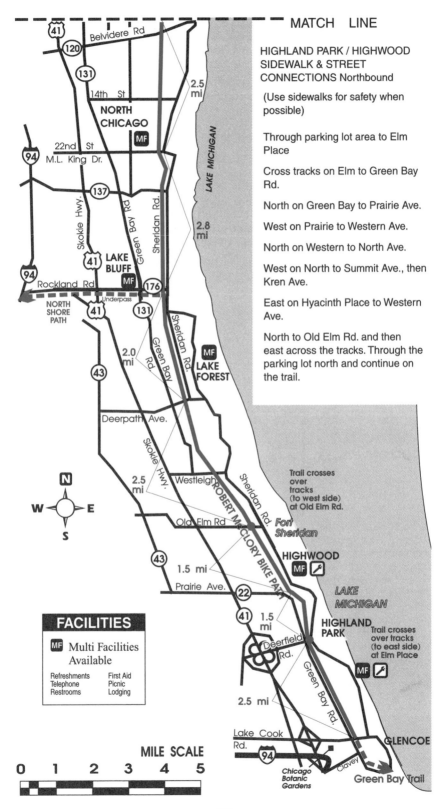

HIGHLAND PARK / HIGHWOOD SIDEWALK & STREET CONNECTIONS Northbound

(Use sidewalks for safety when possible)

Through parking lot area to Elm Place

Cross tracks on Elm to Green Bay Rd.

North on Green Bay to Prairie Ave.

West on Prairie to Western Ave.

North on Western to North Ave.

West on North to Summit Ave., then Kren Ave.

East on Hyacinth Place to Western Ave.

North to Old Elm Rd. and then east across the tracks. Through the parking lot north and continue on the trail.

41
120
Belvidere Rd
131
14th St
2.5 mi
NORTH CHICAGO
MF
22nd St
M.L. King Dr.
94
137
LAKE MICHIGAN
2.8 mi
Skokie Hwy.
Green Bay Rd
Sheridan Rd.
41 LAKE BLUFF
MF
94
Rockland Rd
176
Underpass
NORTH SHORE PATH
41
131
Green Bay Rd.
Sheridan Rd.
2.0 mi
43
MF LAKE FOREST

Deerpath Ave.

N
W E
S

Skokie Hwy.
2.5 mi
Westleigh
Old Elm Rd
ROBERT McCLORY BIKE PATH
Sheridan Rd.
Fort Sheridan

Trail crosses over tracks (to west side) at Old Elm Rd.

43
1.5 mi
Prairie Ave.
22
41
1.5 mi
Deerfield Rd.

HIGHWOOD
MF

LAKE MICHIGAN

HIGHLAND PARK

Trail crosses over tracks (to east side) at Elm Place

MF

Green Bay Rd.

2.5 mi

Lake Cook Rd.
94
Chicago Botanic Gardens
Clavey
GLENCOE
Green Bay Trail

FACILITIES

MF Multi Facilities Available

Refreshments | First Aid
Telephone | Picnic
Restrooms | Lodging

MILE SCALE

0 1 2 3 4 5

Rock Island State Trail

8-31 rode from Toulon to Princeville — enjoyed the ammenities + scenery

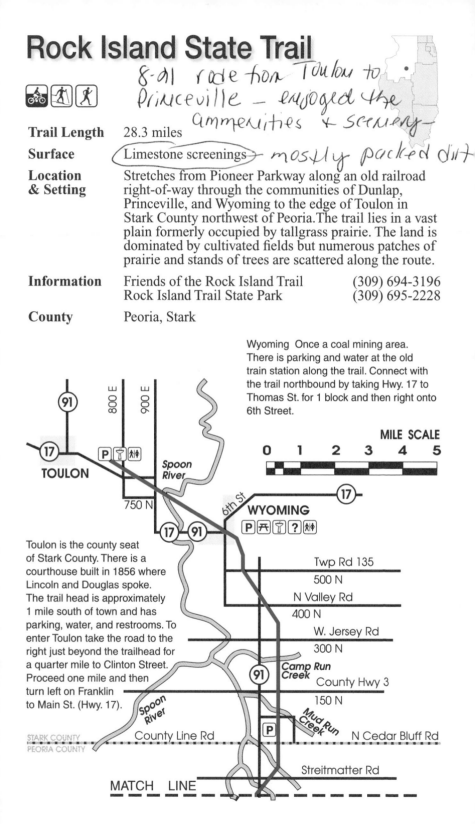

Trail Length	28.3 miles
Surface	~~Limestone screenings~~ *mostly packed dirt*
Location & Setting	Stretches from Pioneer Parkway along an old railroad right-of-way through the communities of Dunlap, Princeville, and Wyoming to the edge of Toulon in Stark County northwest of Peoria. The trail lies in a vast plain formerly occupied by tallgrass prairie. The land is dominated by cultivated fields but numerous patches of prairie and stands of trees are scattered along the route.
Information	Friends of the Rock Island Trail (309) 694-3196 Rock Island Trail State Park (309) 695-2228
County	Peoria, Stark

Wyoming Once a coal mining area. There is parking and water at the old train station along the trail. Connect with the trail northbound by taking Hwy. 17 to Thomas St. for 1 block and then right onto 6th Street.

MILE SCALE

0 1 2 3 4 5

800 E

900 E

91

17

TOULON

Spoon River

750 N

17 91

6th St

WYOMING

Twp Rd 135

500 N

N Valley Rd

400 N

W. Jersey Rd

300 N

Toulon is the county seat of Stark County. There is a courthouse built in 1856 where Lincoln and Douglas spoke. The trail head is approximately 1 mile south of town and has parking, water, and restrooms. To enter Toulon take the road to the right just beyond the trailhead for a quarter mile to Clinton Street. Proceed one mile and then turn left on Franklin to Main St. (Hwy. 17).

Spoon River

91

Camp Run Creek
County Hwy 3

150 N

Mud Run Creek

P

County Line Rd

N Cedar Bluff Rd

STARK COUNTY
PEORIA COUNTY

Streitmatter Rd

MATCH   LINE

140

Other features of The Rock Island Trail include:
An arched culvert with wing wall construction of massive limestone blocks, located about 2 miles north of Alta. A steel trestle bridge, circa 1910, spanning the Spoon River. A rehabilitated rail station in Wyoming, which was built in 1871.

FACILITIES

🔧 Bike Repair
❓ Info
🅿 Parking
🏕 Picnic
🚻 Restrooms
💧 Water
MF Multi Facilities Available

Refreshments	First Aid
Telephone	Picnic
Restrooms	Lodging

ROUTES

━━━━ Bicycling Trail
━━━━ Roadway

PRINCEVILLE You cross the Santa Fe railroad tracks as you enter the town from the south. Just beyond the tracks is a park with restrooms and a picnic area. The trail connects through city streets- proceed on Walnut to North Ave. a short distance and left onto North Town Rd. for a half mile. Turn left on a marked single lane road to connect with the trail again.

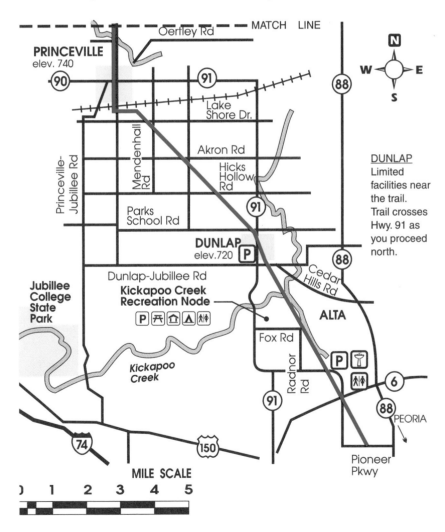

Rock Cut State Park

Trail Length	23 miles
Surface	Dirt
Location & Setting	Located in Winnebago County northeast of Rockford, and approximately 80 miles northwest of Chicago. From I-90, exit at East Riverside Blvd. and head west for 1 mile, then turn right on McFarland Road to Harlem Road (dead end). Turn east (right) for a little over a mile, over I-90, to the Park entrance. Terrain is rugged, rocky with woods and small hills.

Information	Rock Cut State Park	(815) 885-3311
	Emergency	911
County	Winnebago	

There are individual routes for hiking, bicycling, horseback riding and snowmobiling. The track varies from 5 to 10 feet wide.

Rock Cut State Park consists of 3,096 acres. Facilities include concessions, restrooms, water, boat rental and canoe access.

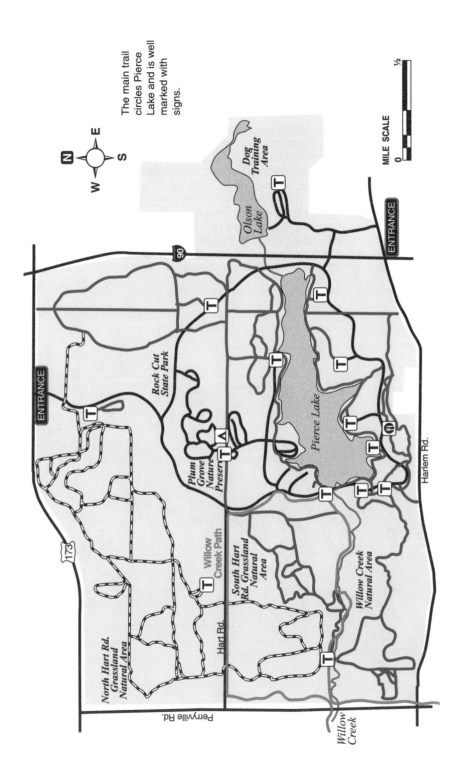

The main trail circles Pierce Lake and is well marked with signs.

MILE SCALE

0   ½

143

Rock Run Greenway

Trail Length	7 miles
Surface	Asphalt
Location & Setting	This 7 mile asphalt paved trail is located in Will County. The Preserve, once wetland, is now being restored. It extends from 1.5 miles from Theodore Marsh on Theodore Street in Crest Hill south and west. From there it loops through to Black Road for 1.4 miles. Pick up the trail again at Jefferson for another 4 miles to the I&M Canal Access, and Joliet Junior College. Open hours are from 8 am to 8 pm. There is an entrance on the west side of Essington Road at Ingalls Avenue, and off the north side of Black Road west of Essington Road.
Information	Forest Preserve District of Will County (815) 727-8700
County	Will

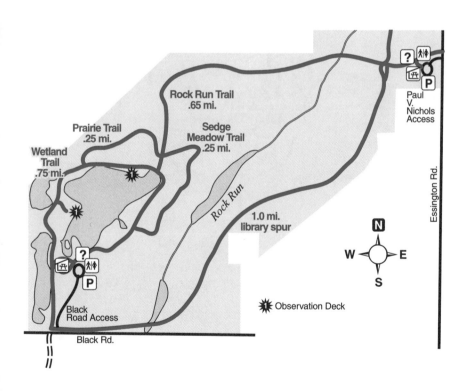

Rock Run Trail
.65 mi.

Prairie Trail
.25 mi.

Sedge
Meadow Trail
.25 mi.

Wetland
Trail
.75 mi.

Rock Run

1.0 mi.
library spur

Paul
V.
Nichols
Access

Essington Rd.

Black
Road Access

Black Rd.

※ Observation Deck

Rock River & Sportscore Recreation Path

Trail Length	8 miles
Surface	Asphalt
Location & Setting	The path follows the Rock River in Rockford from Walnut Street north through Veterans Memorial Park/ Sportscore to Harlem Road. The setting is urban.
Information	Rockford Park District (815) 987-8800
County	Winnebago

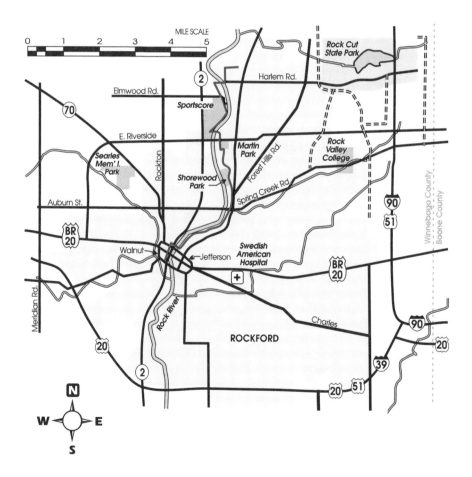

The Sportscore joins the Rock River Path at Elmwood Road, proceeds along Brown Beach Road jogging west, then northeast along Harlem Road and across the Rock River. The path crosses the Rock River at Jefferson Street, Riverside Blvd. and Harlem Road. There are numerous points of interest along the path.

Rollins Savanna
Forest Preserve

Trail Length	7 miles
Surface	Crushed stone
Location & Setting	Rollins Savanna offers over 7.2 miles of 12 foot-wide gravel trail with bridges and boardwalks for biking, hiking and wildlife observation, and .7 miles of 8 foot-wide gravel educational trail loop. It contains scattered groves of majestic oaks, wide-open prairies teeming with wildflowers, native grasses and abundant wetlands. Facilities include drinking water, restrooms, trailside nature education exhibits and observation blinds. The preserve is open from 6:30 a.m. to sunset. The main entrance is off Washington Street across from Atkinson Road, about .2 miles east of Route 83 and 1.4 miles west of Route 45.
Information	Lake County Forest Preserves (847) 367-6640
County	Lake

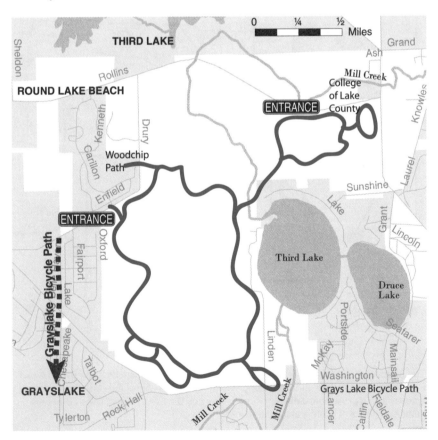

Running Deer Trail

Trail Length	3 miles
Surface	Natural
Location & Setting	The trail is located in Dirksen Park, north of Pekin and Rte 98. It consists of some 600 acres of woodland and meadows. At its highest point it overlooks the Illinois River Valley. The trailhead is on the north side of Route 98, at McNaughton Park Road. Parking is available south of the Archery Range Road on Route 98 and along Pontiac Road in Marquette Heights.
Information	Pekin Park District (309) 347-7275
County	Tazewell

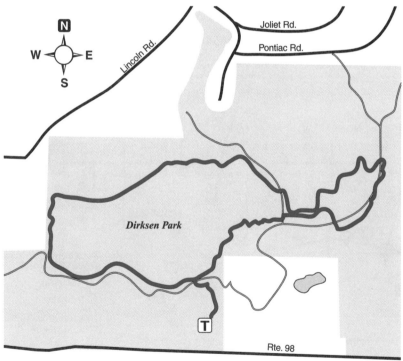

McNaughton Park

Salt Creek Bicycle Trail

Trail Length	6.6 miles
Surface	Paved
Location & Setting	Located in west central Cook County. Bordered clockwise by the communities of Oakbrook, Westchester, Brookfield, LaGrange Park, LaGrange and Hinsdale. The Salt Creek Trail starts in Bemis Woods South and continues east to Brookfield Woods, directly across from the Brookfield Zoo. As the trail follows Salt Creek, it provides access to various picnic groves and other points of interest. The trail may be accessed from Ogden Avenue, just east of Wolf Road, or from 31st Street between First Avenue and Prairie Avenue.
Information	Forest Preserve District of Cook County (708) 366-9420 Emergency Assistance (708) 366-8210
County	Cook

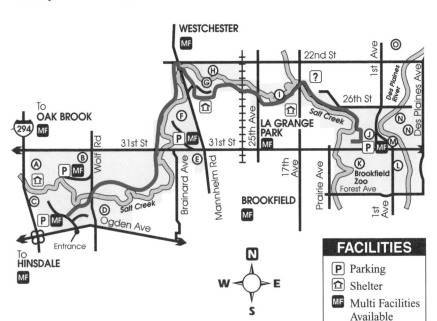

POINTS OF INTEREST

A. Meadow Lark Golf Course
B. Bemis Woods North
C. Bemis Woods South
D. Salt Creek Nursery
E. La Grange Park Woods
F. Possum Hollow Woods
G. Brezina Woods
H. Westchester Woods

I. 26th Street Woods
J. Brookfield Woods
K. Brookfield Zoo
L. Zoo Woods
M. McCormick Woods
N. National Grove-North & South
O. Miller Meadows

FACILITIES

P Parking
Shelter
MF Multi Facilities Available

Refreshments   First Aid
Telephone   Picnic
Restrooms   Lodging

Skokie Valley Trail

Trail Length	6.5 miles
Surface	Asphalt
Location & Setting	The Skokie Valley Trial runs north and south between Old Elm Road in Lake Forest south to West Park in Highland Park. The trail parallels the west side of Hwy 41 (Old Skokie Hwy) and is built on ComEd right-of-way. There is an overpass at Half Day Road (Hwy 22). Northcroft Park provides parking and easy access, and is located on the southwest side of the Old Elm Road and Hwy 41 intersections.
Information	Lake County Division of Transportation (847) 362-3950
County	Lake

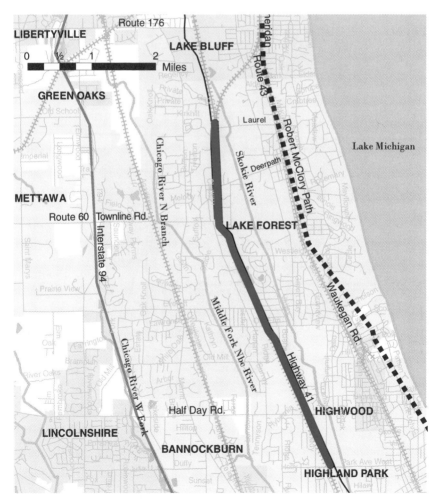

Springbrook Prairie

Trail Length	8.5 miles
Surface	Limestone screening, mowed turf
Location & Setting	Springbrook Prairie is a newly developed 1,878 acre preserve with 8.5 miles of trail. Much of this previous farmland is in the process of being restored to native grasses, creating a savanna-like setting. Drinking water, flush toilets, shelters and picnic areas are located throughout the preserve. There are over 6 miles of crushed limestone trail and 2 miles of narrow, mowed trail. Located in Naperville. There are entrances off Plainfield/Naperville Road, between 75th Street and 87th Street.
Information	Forest Preserve District of DuPage County (630) 933-7200
County	DuPage

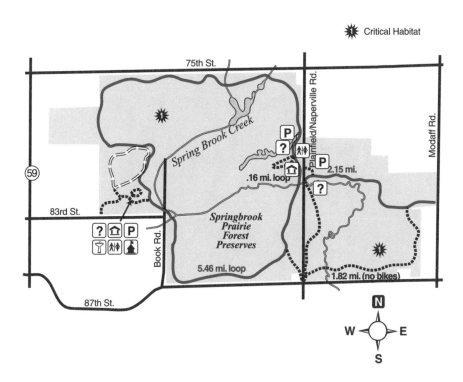

Stone Bridge Trail

Trail Length	5.75 miles
Surface	Screenings
Location & Setting	The trail is built on an abandoned railbed and begins at McCurry Road in Roscoe then proceeds southeast to the Boone county line. The setting is rural with wide open areas and farmland.
Information	Rockford Park District (815) 987-8865
County	Winnebago

The Stone Bridge Trail joins the Long Prairie Trail at the Boone County line.

ROUTES

▬▬▬	Bicycling Trail
= = =	Planned Trail
▬▬▬	Roadway

FACILITIES

P Parking
MF Multi Facilities Available

Refreshments   First Aid
Telephone   Picnic
Restrooms   Lodging

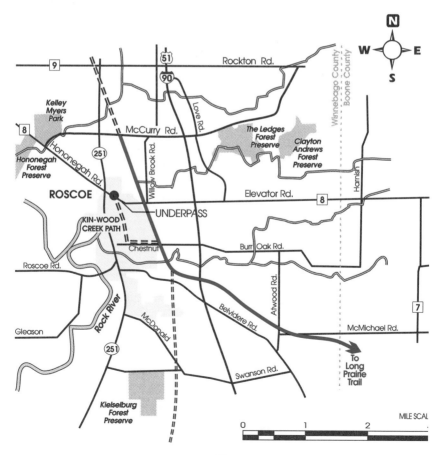

Sugar Creek Preserve (Wauponsee Glacial Trail)

Trail Length	26 miles
Surface	Asphalt, crushed limestone
Location & Setting	The Wauponsee Glacial Trail, located in the Sugar Creek Preserve, is a 26 miles trail following abandoned rail lines from Joliet to Kankakee. The trail north of Laraway Road will be asphalt for 3.3 miles. South of Laraway Road, the trail will be surfaced with limestone screenings. The 8 mile segment from Joliet to Manhattan has been completed. Preserve hours are 8 am to 8 pm. The Sugar Creek Preserve is located at 17540 West Laraway Road, approximately .75 miles west of Rte. 52 in Joliet.
Information	Forest Preserve District of Will County (815) 727-8700
County	Will

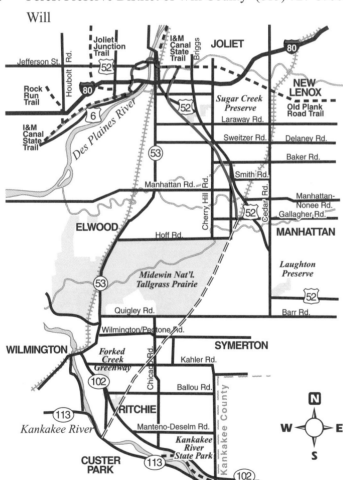

Thorn Creek
Forest Preserve

Trail Length	9.3 miles
Surface	Paved
Location & Setting	The Thorn Creek Bicycle Trail is located in far south Cook County. One section consists of trail through the Sauk Trail lake area and another winds through Lansing Woods and North Creek Meadow. A future extension will link these sections. Access the western section along Ashland Avenue, and the eastern section from either Glenwood-Lansing Road or 183rd Street east of Torrence Avenue. It is bounded clockwise by the communities of South Holland, Lansing, Chicago Heights, South Chicago Heights, Park Forest, Olympia Fields, Glenwood and Thornton.
Information	Forest Preserve District of Cook County (708)366-9420
County	Cook

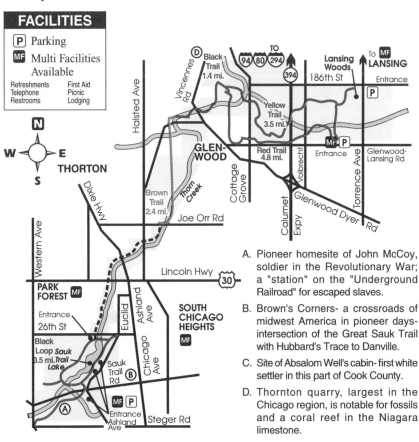

FACILITIES

P Parking

MF Multi Facilities Available

Refreshments First Aid
Telephone Picnic
Restrooms Lodging

N
W E
S

THORTON

Halsted Ave
Vincennes Rd

D Black Trail 1.4 mi.

TO
94 80 294
394

Lansing Woods
186th St

To MF
LANSING

Entrance
P

Yellow Trail 3.5 mi.

GLEN-WOOD

Red Trail 4.8 mi.

MF P
Entrance

Glenwood-Lansing Rd

Volbrecht

Torrence Ave

Cottage Grove

Dixie Hwy

Thorn Creek

Brown Trail 2.4 mi.

Joe Orr Rd

Calumet Expy

Glenwood Dyer Rd

Western Ave

Lincoln Hwy
30

PARK FOREST MF

Entrance 26th St

Euclid

Ashland Ave

SOUTH CHICAGO HEIGHTS
MF

Black Loop Sauk 3.5 mi. Trail Lake

Sauk Trail Rd B

Chicago Ave

MF P
Entrance Ashland Ave

Steger Rd

A

A. Pioneer homesite of John McCoy, soldier in the Revolutionary War; a "station" on the "Underground Railroad" for escaped slaves.

B. Brown's Corners- a crossroads of midwest America in pioneer days- intersection of the Great Sauk Trail with Hubbard's Trace to Danville.

C. Site of Absalom Well's cabin- first white settler in this part of Cook County.

D. Thornton quarry, largest in the Chicago region, is notable for fossils and a coral reef in the Niagara limestone.

Tinley Creek
Forest Preserve

Trail Length	23.5 miles
Surface	Paved
Location & Setting	The Tinley Creek Bicycle Trail is located in southwestern Cook County. The trail passes through gently rolling country, forests, prairies and alongside wetlands. It is bordered (clockwise) by the communities of Palos Heights, Crestwood, Oak Forest, Country Club Hills, Flossmoor, Tinley Park and Orland Park.
Information	Forest Preserve District of Cook County (708) 366-9420 Forest Preserve Police Emergency Assistance (708) 366-8210
County	Cook

Pause along 159th Street, just east of Oak Park Avenue, for an unusual view of the Chicago skyline, approximately 20 miles to the northeast. There are accesses and parking along Central Avenue between 159th Street and 175th Street in the northern section. Access and parking to the southern loop is available off both Vollmer and Flossmoor Roads. A future extension will link these two sections.

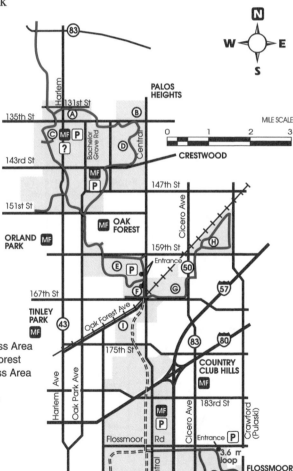

A. Arrowhead Lake Access Area
B. Elizabeth A. Conkey Forest
C. Turtlehead Lake Access Area
D. Rubio Woods
E. The George W. Dunne National Golf Course
F. Yankee Woods
G. Midlothian Reservoir (Twin Lakes)
H. Midlothian Meadows
I. St. Mihiel West
J. Vollmer Road Picnic

Riding the Des Plaines Division Trail

Tunnel Hill State Trail

Trail Length	45 miles
Surface	Crushed stone
Location & Setting	The Tunnel Hill Trail, when completed, will extend over 44 miles connecting the towns of Harrisburg to the north with Karnak to the south. It is being built on old railbed. Facilities are available at most of the 8 communities along its route. The trail parallels the west side of Hwy 45 south to Bloomfield, where it crosses to the east, then west again 3 miles south of Vienna paralleling Hwy 3 to Karnak.
Information	Tunnel Hill State Trail (618)658-2168
	Shawnee National Forest Forest Supervisor (800) MY WOODS (699-6637)
County	Saline, Williamson and Johnson

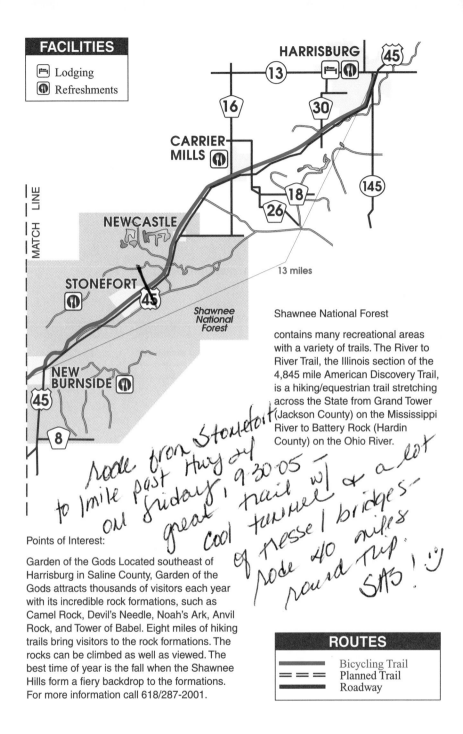

HARRISBURG

CARRIER MILLS

NEWCASTLE

STONEFORT

NEW BURNSIDE

13 miles

Shawnee National Forest

Shawnee National Forest

contains many recreational areas with a variety of trails. The River to River Trail, the Illinois section of the 4,845 mile American Discovery Trail, is a hiking/equestrian trail stretching across the State from Grand Tower (Jackson County) on the Mississippi River to Battery Rock (Hardin County) on the Ohio River.

rode from Stonefort to 1mile past Hwy 34 on Friday, 9-30-05 great trail. cool tunnel w/ a lot of nessel bridges- rode 40 miles round trip. SAS! :)

Points of Interest:

Garden of the Gods Located southeast of Harrisburg in Saline County, Garden of the Gods attracts thousands of visitors each year with its incredible rock formations, such as Camel Rock, Devil's Needle, Noah's Ark, Anvil Rock, and Tower of Babel. Eight miles of hiking trails bring visitors to the rock formations. The rocks can be climbed as well as viewed. The best time of year is the fall when the Shawnee Hills form a fiery backdrop to the formations. For more information call 618/287-2001.

ROUTES

━━━━ Bicycling Trail
= = = Planned Trail
━━━━ Roadway

Vadalabene Bike Trail

Trail Length	19 miles
Surface	Paved
Location & Setting	This path follows Route 100 between Alton, through Grafton and to Pere Marquette State Park. The bikeway is bordered by towering limestone cliffs and the Mississippi River, and is a recreational destination for bicycle enthusiasts.
Information	Illinois Dept. of Transportation (618) 346-3100
	Southern Illinois Tourism Council Box 286 Belleville, IL 62222
County	Madison, Jersey

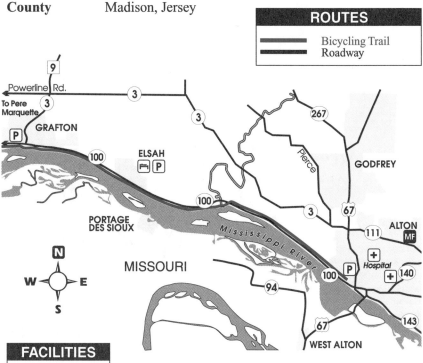

ROUTES

━━━ Bicycling Trail
━━━ Roadway

FACILITIES

➕ First Aid
🛏 Lodging
🅿 Parking
MF Multi Facilities Available

Refreshments   First Aid
Telephone   Picnic
Restrooms   Lodging

The northern section follows the wide paved shoulders of the McAdams Parkway to Grafton. The southern section is a separate paved path built on an abandoned railroad line at the base of the bluffs. There are parking areas along and at each end of the bikeway. Pause to visit the historic town of Grafton and Elsah with their antique shops.

Vernon Hills Trails

Trail Length	7.0 miles
Surface	Paved
Location & Setting	Vernon Hills is located in central Lake County.

Century Park	**Deerpath**
Route 60 west ¾ miles of Route 21 to Lakeview Parkway. Turn north for ½ mile to the park.	Route 60 past Lakeview Parkway to Deerpath Drive. Turn south and proceed to Cherokee Road. Turn east (left) to Deerpath Park.

Information	Vernon Hills Park District	(847) 367-7270
County	Lake	

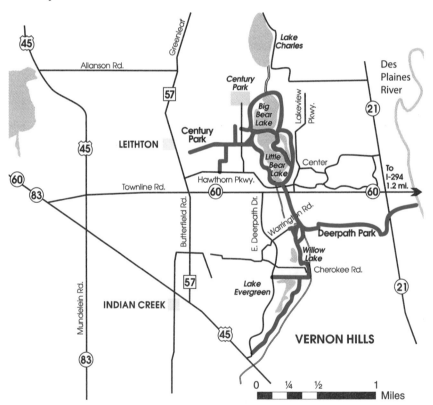

Open field and some woods. ExercisAe stations surround the lake in Century Park. The path runs through Deerpath Park playgrounds, tennis courts and a small lake.

Veteran Acres Park

Trail Length	Approximately 7.5 miles
Surface	Natural
Location & Setting	Located on the north side of Crystal Lake. Access from Terra Cotta Road from the south or Walkup Road from the west.
Information	Crystal Lake Park District (815) 459-0680
County	McHenry

Sterne's Woods can be accessed from Veteran Acres and has about two miles of dirt road open to hiking.

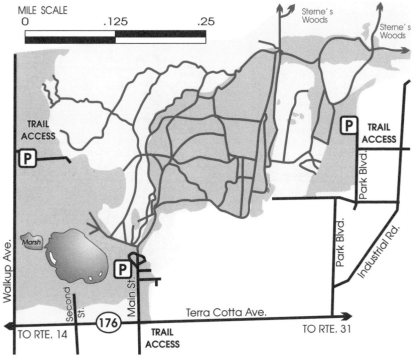

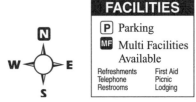

Virgil L. Gilman Nature Trail

Trail Length	10.5 miles
Surface	Paved
Location & Setting	The trail stretches west uninterrupted past farmlands straddling the Kane and Kendall County border. The Virgil Gilman Trail passes rural, urban and suburban areas.
Information	Fox River Park District (630) 897-0516
County	Kane

The rural landscape gives way to city life when entering Aurora.

Aurora is the largest community in Kane County. It was the first midwest community to electrically illuminate its streets.

Services are available at Parker Avenue, Elmwood Drive, Orchard Road, Blackberry Village and Bliss Woods.

FACILITIES

- 🔧 Bike Repair
- ➕ First Aid
- 🏳 Lodging
- P Parking
- ⛱ Picnic
- 🚻 Restrooms
- **MF** Multi Facilities Available

Refreshments	First Aid
Telephone	Picnic
Restrooms	Lodging

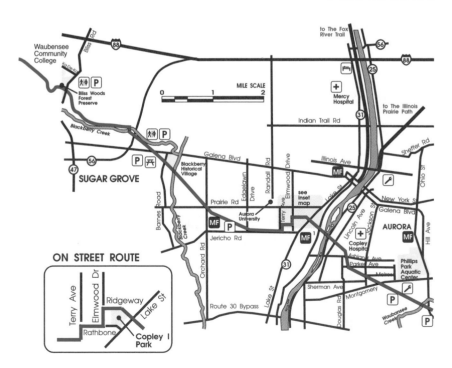

Waterfall Glen Forest Preserve

Trail Length   11.7 miles

Surface   Limestone screenings

Location & Setting   Southeast corner of DuPage County, the trail circles Argonne National Laboratory. Forests, prairie, open areas.

Information   Forest Preserve District of DuPage County (630) 933-7200

County   DuPage

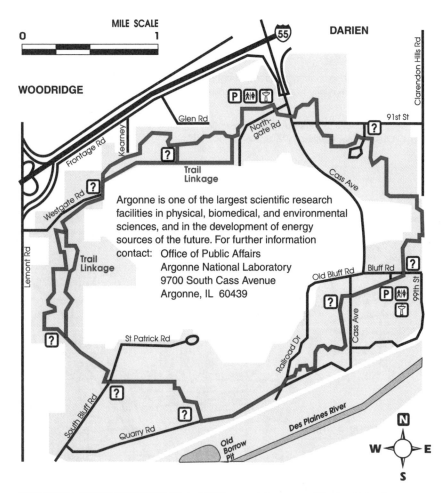

Argonne is one of the largest scientific research facilities in physical, biomedical, and environmental sciences, and in the development of energy sources of the future. For further information contact: Office of Public Affairs
Argonne National Laboratory
9700 South Cass Avenue
Argonne, IL 60439

WATERFALL GLEN PRESERVE Waterfall Glen provides some of the best bicycling, cross country skiing and hiking in DuPage County. The main trail is 8 feet wide. In addition, there are many mowed grass trails and footpaths through the preserve.

Zion Bicycle Path

Trail Length	6.5 miles
Surface	Paved
Uses	Leisure bicycling, in-line skating, jogging
Location & Setting	This bicycle path and bikeway is located in the community of Zion in far northeastern Illinois. The setting is surburban.
Information	Zion Park District (847) 746-5500
County	Lake

ROUTES

———— Bicycling Trail
━ ━ ━ Bikeway
▬ ▪ ▬ Alternate Bike Trail
━━━━ Roadway

There is a trail extension planned that will run west along the Commonwealth Edison right-of-way (near Hwy. 173) to the Highland Meadows development.

FACILITIES

? Info
P Parking
⊼ Picnic
◍ Refreshments
⋔ Restrooms
🛈 Water
MF Multi Facilities Available

Refreshments   First Aid
Telephone   Picnic
Restrooms   Lodging

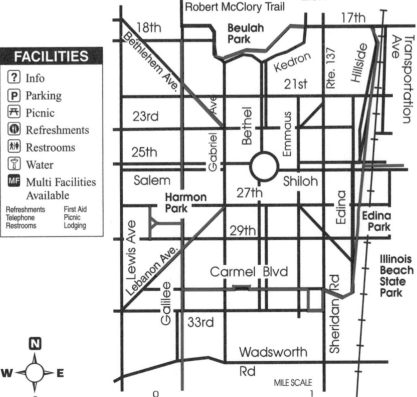

Find me a place, safe and serene,

away from the terror I see on the screen.

A place where my soul can find some peace,

away from the stress and the pressures released.

A corridor of green not far from my home

for fresh air and exercise, quiet will roam.

Summer has smells that tickle my nose

and fall has the leaves that crunch under my toes.

Beware, comes a person we pass in a while

with a wave and hello and a wide friendly smile.

Recreation trails are the place to be,

to find that safe haven of peace and serenity.

By Beverly Moore, Illinois Trails Conservancy

Additional Trails

BARTLETT'S TRAILS & BIKEWAYS 🚲🚶

Trail Length   15 miles
Location & Setting Bartlett. There is a trailhead on Route 50 between Routes
                              59 and 43 and at the intersection of Routes 59 and 6.
Information   Bartlett Park District   (630) 837-6568
County   Cook

BELLEVILLE'S TRAILS & BIKEWAYS 🚲🚶

Trail Length   6 miles
Surface   Crushed stone
                              East Belleville. Trailheads at the junction of Routes 44
Location & Setting and 89 and the junction of Routes 158 and 159.
Information   Belleville Chamber of Commerce   (618) 233-2077
County   St. Clair

CHAIN OF LAKES BIKE PATH 🚲🚶⛸

Trail Length   3 miles
Surface   Asphalt
Location & Setting This trail parallels the south side of Rollins Rd in Fox
                              Lake. It runs from Sayton Rd eastward to where it connects
                              to the Grant Woods Forest Preserve Trail, .8 miles east of
                              Wilson Rd. There is an underpass at Route 59, but it's a road
                              crossing at Wilson Rd. From the east take Belvidere Rd (Route 120)
                              to Cedar Lake Rd, then north to Rollins Rd.
Information   Lake County Dept. of Transportation   (847) 382-3750
County   Lake

DEKALB/SYCAMORE TRAIL 🚲🚶🚴

Trail Length   6 miles
Surface   Paved
Location & Setting The DeKalb/Sycamore Trail is 6 miles long, paved, and
                              links the DeKalb Park District Trail from Lions Park on
                              DeKalb's south side to Sycamore and the Great Western Trail.
Information   DeKalb County Forest Preserve   (815) 895-7191
County   DeKalb

EL PASO TRAIL 🚲🚶

Trail Length   2.7 miles
Surface   Crushed stone
Location & Setting Town of El Paso
Information   City Hall   (309) 527-4005
                              52 North Elm, El Paso, IL 61738-4005
County   Madison

GREEN DIAMOND RAIL TRAIL 🚲🚶⛸🎿

Trail Length   4 miles
Surface   Asphalt
Location & Setting A flat, easy trail located in Montgomery County, and built
                              on abandoned Illinois Central railroad corridor. There is trail
                              access at the south end of Cleveland Street in Farmersville and
                              at the Historic Depot Park on Main Street in Waggoner.
Information   Montgomery County Coordinator   217-532-9577
County   Montgomery

Additional Trails (continued)

HERITAGE-DONNELLEY TRAIL

Trail Length	5 miles
Surface	Paved
Location & Setting	A 5 mile paved trail running between Joliet and Lockport, forming part of the I&M Canal corridor.
Information	Will County Forest Preserve (815) 727-8700
County	Will

HUMPHREY TRAIL

Trail Length	3 miles
Surface	Paved
Location & Setting	The John Humphrey Trail is located in Orland Park, and connects the Village Center and Metra station. It's 3 miles long and surfaced. The setting is urban, with woods and nearby wetlands.
Information	Orland Park District (708) 403-6115
County	Cook

INTERURBAN TRAIL

Trail Length	7 miles
Surface	Asphalt
Location & Setting	The Interurban Trail was built on abandoned Interurban Railroad Right-of-Way in Springfield. It begins at the corner of Wabash Avenue and MacArthur Blvd., and proceeds in a southerly direction to Woodside Road.
Information	Springfield Park District (217) 544-1751
County	Sangamon

JOE STENGEL TRAIL

Trail Length	11 miles
Surface	Natural
Location & Setting	The 11 mile Joe Stengel Trail links Dixon & Polo using natural surface trails and roadways. The Polo trailhead is located off Judson Road.
Information	Dixon Park District (815) 284-3308
County	Ogle, Lee

LAKE OF THE WOODS TRAIL

Trail Length	4 miles
Surface	Paved
Location & Setting	The Lake of the Woods Trail is paved, and is located 10 miles west of Champaign-Urbana on I-74 at Mahomet, exit #172 or #174. It passes the Early American Museum and Botanical Garden.
Information	Champaign County Forest Preserve (217) 586-3360
County	Champaign

LYONS WOODS FOREST PRESERVE

Trail Length	3 miles
Surface	Crushed granite
Location & Setting	This preserve offers a diverse mix or prairie, savanna, pine grove, forest and fen. Lyons Woods is near Waukegan and Beach Park. From downtown Waukegan, take Sheridan Rd. north to Blanchard Rd. and turn left for a short distance to the entrance.
Information	Lake County Forest Preserve (847) 367-6640
County	Lake

MALLARD LAKE FOREST PRESERVE

Trail Length	3.7 miles
Surface	Groomed
Location & Setting	The Mallard Lake Forest Preserve winds through and over a mixture of habitats including open water, grassy fields and scattered woodlands. The trail can be accessed from the parking area and will lead you through the preserve's picnic area and around and across Mallard Lake over two bridges. The terrain is relatively level and trail surface is limestone screenings and mowed turf. Located in Bloomingdale off the intersection of Lawrence Ave. and Cloverdale Rd.
Information	Forest Preserve District of DuPage County (630) 933-7300
County	DuPage

NEWTON LAKE FISH & WILDLIFE AREA

Trail Length	4.5 miles
Surface	Natural
Location & Setting	4.5 mile biking trail located SW of Newton in southern IL. From Newton; S on 1100E to 700N, W to 300N, S to 500N, then E to the entrance.
Information	Newton Lake Fish & Wildlife Area (618) 783-3478
County	Jasper

PIONEER PARKWAY

Trail Length	2.5 miles
Surface	Crushed stone
Location & Setting	From Peoria to Alta
Information	Peoria Park District (309) 682-1200
County	Peoria

TRI-COUNTY TRAIL

Trail Length	4 miles
Surface	Groomed
Location & Setting	Owned by the Illinois DNR and operated by the FP District of DuPage County, the Tri-County trail offers more than 4 miles of multipurpose trails that meander through some of the park's most scenic areas, including remnants of tall grass prairie. The trail surface is limestone screenings. Located in Bartlett off Stearns Road, west of Dunham Road.
Information	Forest Preserve District of DuPage County(630) 933-7200
County	DuPage

WAUBONSIE TRAIL

Trail Length	2.5 miles
Surface	Paved
Location & Setting	Town of Oswego, S of Aurora. Surface is asphalt, setting urban parkland.
Information	Oswego Park District (630) 554-1010
County	Kendall

Selected Illinois State Parks

North West Region

North West Region Park Name	Acreage	Concession	Drinking Water	Rest rooms	Bike Trails	Boat Rentals	Canoe Access	Canoe Rental	Hiking	Camping
			FACILITIES				ACTIVITIES			
Argyle Lake State Park	1700	●	●	♿		●	●		●	AB/CDY
Big River State Forest	3027	♿	♿				●		●	CD
Castle Rock State Park	1995	●	●				●		●	Canoe
Delabar State Park	89	●	●				●		●	B/ECD
Hennepin Canal Parkway State Park	5773	♿	♿		●		●		♿	CDY
Ilini State Park	510	●	●	♿			●		●	B/ECY
Johnson-Sauk Trail State Park	1361	●	♿	♿		●	●		●	B/E♿DY
Jubilee College State Park	3500	♿	♿						●	AB/SC♿
Lake Le-Aqua-Na State Park	715	●	●	♿		●	●		♿	AB/SCY
Lowden State Park	2234	●	♿	♿			●		●	AB/SD
Mississippi Palisades State Park	2505	●	●	♿			●		●	AB/SDY A♿
Rock Cut State Park	3092	●	♿	♿	●	●	●		●	B/SCY
Rock Island Trail State Park	392	♿	♿	●					●	D
Starved Rock State Park	2630	♿	♿	♿			●		●	A♿YL
White Pines Forest State Park	385	♿	●	♿					●	CY

CLASS **A** SITES — Showers, electricity & vehicular access *(fee)*

CLASS **B/E** SITES — Electricity & vehicular access *(fee)*

CLASS **B/S** SITES — Showers & vehicular access *(fee)*

CLASS **C** SITES — Vehicular access *(fee)*

CLASS **D** SITES — Tent camping/primitive sites (walk in/backpack) no vehicular access *(fee)*

CLASS **Y** SITES — Youth Groups only

♿ — Accessible to visitors with disabilities

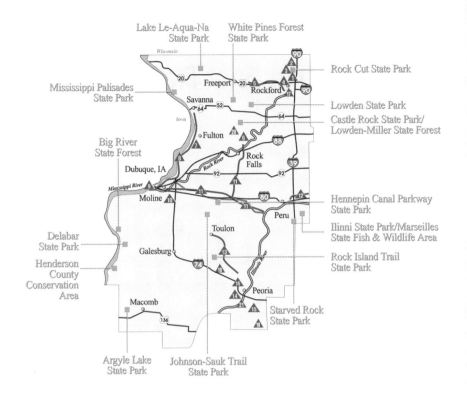

Lake Le-Aqua-Na State Park

White Pines Forest State Park

Rock Cut State Park

Mississippi Palisades State Park

Lowden State Park

Castle Rock State Park/ Lowden-Miller State Forest

Big River State Forest

Dubuque, IA

Delabar State Park

Henderson County Conservation Area

Hennepin Canal Parkway State Park

Ilinni State Park/Marseilles State Fish & Wildlife Area

Rock Island Trail State Park

Starved Rock State Park

Argyle Lake State Park

Johnson-Sauk Trail State Park

Selected Illinois State Parks

North East Region

North East Region Park Name	FACILITIES				ACTIVITIES					
	Acreage	Concession	Drinking Water	Rest rooms	Bike Trails	Boat Rentals	Canoe Access	Canoe Rental	Hiking	Camping
Chain O'Lakes State Park	6063	●	♿	♿	●	●	●	●		AB/SY
Channahon State Park	25		●	●	●		●		●	DY
Des Plaines Conservation Area	5012	●	●	♿			●		●	C
Gebhard Woods State Park	30		♿	●			●		●	DY
Goose Lake Prairie State Nat'l. Area	2468		●	♿					●	
I & M Canal State Trail	2802		●	●	●		●		●	D
Illinois Beach State Park	4160	♿	♿	♿	●		●		♿	A&YL
Kankakee River State Park	3932	♿	♿	♿	●		●	●	●	A&B/ECDY
Moraine Hills State Park	1763	●	♿	●	●	●			●	
Silver Springs State Park	1314	●	●	♿			●	●	●	DY

CLASS **A** SITES — Showers, electricity & vehicular access *(fee)*

CLASS **B/E** SITES — Electricity & vehicular access *(fee)*

CLASS **B/S** SITES — Showers & vehicular access *(fee)*

CLASS **C** SITES — Vehicular access *(fee)*

CLASS **D** SITES — Tent camping/primitive sites (walk in/backpack) no vehicular access *(fee)*

CLASS **Y** SITES — Youth Groups only

♿ — Accessible to visitors with disabilities

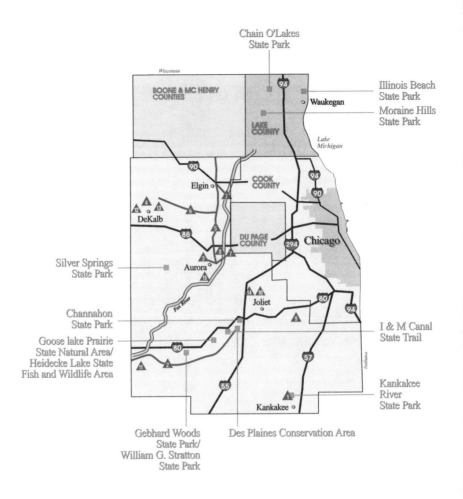

Selected Illinois State Parks

East Central Region

East Central Region Park Name	FACILITIES				ACTIVITIES					
	Acreage	Concession	Drinking Water	Rest rooms	Bike Trails	Boat Rentals	Canoe Access	Canoe Rental	Hiking	Camping
Clinton Lake State Recreation Area	9915		ᕗ	ᕗ		●			●	B/SY
Eagle Creek State Recreation Area	1463	●		ᕗ					●	B/ECY
Fox Ridge State Park	1517	●		ᕗ					●	B/SY
Hidden Springs State Forest	1121	●		ᕗ					●	CY
Kickapoo State Park	2844	●	●	ᕗ	●	●	●	●	●	AB/SCDYR
Lincoln Trail State Park	1022	ᕗ	●		ᕗ		●	●	●	●	A&DY
Moraine View State Park	1688	ᕗ	ᕗ	ᕗ		●	●			ᕗ	B/ED
Walnut Point State Fish & Wildlife Area	592	●	●	ᕗ		●	●		●	B/EDY
Weldon Springs State Park	370	●	●	ᕗ		●	●		●	B/EDY
Wolf Creek State Park	1967	●		ᕗ					●	RACDY

CLASS **A** SITES — Showers, electricity & vehicular access *(fee)*

CLASS **B/E** SITES — Electricity & vehicular access *(fee)*

CLASS **B/S** SITES — Showers & vehicular access *(fee)*

CLASS **C** SITES — Vehicular access *(fee)*

CLASS **D** SITES — Tent camping/primitive sites (walk in/backpack) no vehicular access *(fee)*

CLASS **Y** SITES — Youth Groups only

ᕗ — Accessible to visitors with disabilities

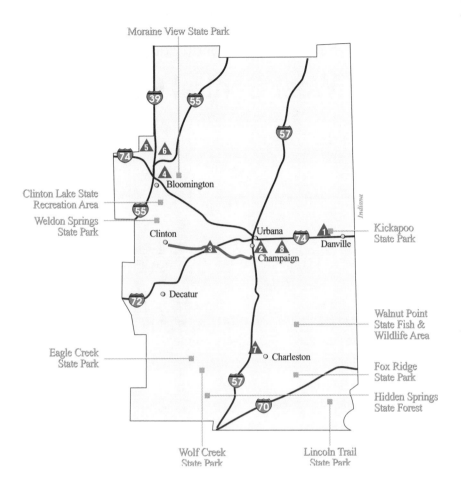

Selected Illinois State Parks

West Central Region

West Central Region Park Name	Acreage	FACILITIES				ACTIVITIES				
		Concession	Drinking Water	Rest rooms	Bike Trails	Boat Rentals	Canoe Access	Canoe Rental	Hiking	Camping
Beaver Dam State Park	744	●	●	♿			●	●	●	AB/SY
Horseshoe Lake State Park	2854		●	♿			●		●	C♿
Nauvoo State Park	148		♿	♿			●			B/ECY
Pere Marquette State Park	7901	●	●	♿	●				●	A&B/SYL
Randolph County State F & W Area	1021	●	●	♿			●	●	●	C&DY
Sand Ridge State Forest	7112		●	●					●	CDY
Sangchris Lake State Park	3576	●		♿			●			B/ECDY
Siloam Springs State Park	3323	♿	♿	♿			●	●	●	A&B/SD
Washington Cnty Conservation Area	1440	♿	♿	♿			●	●	●	A&CY
Weinberg-King State Park	772		●	♿					●	C&Y

CLASS **A** SITES	Showers, electricity & vehicular access *(fee)*
CLASS **B/E** SITES	Electricity & vehicular access *(fee)*
CLASS **B/S** SITES	Showers & vehicular access *(fee)*
CLASS **C** SITES	Vehicular access *(fee)*
CLASS **D** SITES	Tent camping/primitive sites (walk in/backpack) no vehicular access *(fee)*
CLASS **Y** SITES	Youth Groups only
♿	Accessible to visitors with disabilities

Selected Illinois State Parks

South Region

South Region Park Name	FACILITIES				ACTIVITIES					
	Acreage	Concession	Drinking Water	Rest rooms	Bike Trails	Boat Rentals	Canoe Access	Canoe Rental	Hiking	Camping
Cave-in-Rock State Park	204	●	●	♿			●		●	B/ECDY
Dixon Springs State Park	787	♿	♿	♿				●	●	B/ED&Y
Ferne Clyffe State Park	1125		♿	♿					●	ADY
Fort Massac State Park	1499		♿	♿			●		●	A♿B/S
Giant City State Park	3694	♿	♿	♿			●	●	♿	A♿DYL
Hamilton County Conservation Area	1683	●	●	●		●	●		●	B/EDY
Horseshoe Lake Conservation Area	9550		♿	♿			●			A♿B/EC
Lake Murphysboro State Park	1024	♿	●	♿		●	●		●	A/ECY
Pyramid State Park	2528		●	●			●		●	CD
Ramsey Lake State Park	1881	●	●	♿		●	●		●	AB,ECDY
Red Hills State Park	948	●	●	♿		●	●		●	A♿DY
Sam Dale Lake Conservation Area	1301	●	♿	♿		●	●		●	B/ED&Y
Sam Parr State Park	1133		●	●					●	CDY
Trail of Tears State Forest	4993		●	●					●	DCY
Wayne Fitzgerrell State Park	3300	●	●	●		●			●	●	AD

CLASS **A** SITES   Showers, electricity & vehicular access *(fee)*

CLASS **B/E** SITES   Electricity & vehicular access *(fee)*

CLASS **B/S** SITES   Showers & vehicular access *(fee)*

CLASS **C** SITES   Vehicular access *(fee)*

CLASS **D** SITES   Tent camping/primitive sites (walk in/backpack) no vehicular access *(fee)*

CLASS **Y** SITES   Youth Groups only

  ♿   Accessible to visitors with disabilities

Index

Index (continued)

City to Trail Index

City to Trail Index (continued)

City to Trail Index (continued)

City to Trail Index (continued)

POPULATION CODE

❶=under 1,000 ❷=1,000-4,999 ❸=5,000-9,999 ❹=10,000-49,999 ❺=50,000 and over

County to Trail Index

County to Trail Index (continued)

Illinois Bicycle Related Laws

625 ILCS 5/11-1502 TRAFFIC LAWS APPLY TO PERSONS RIDING BICYCLES Every person riding a bicycle upon a highway shall be granted all of the rights and shall be subject to all of the duties applicable to the driver of a vehicle.

625 ILCS 5/11-1503 RIDING ON BICYCLES

    (a) A person propelling a bicycle shall not ride other than upon or astride a permanent and regular seat attached thereto.

    (b) No bicycle shall be used to carry more persons at one time than the number for which it is designed and equipped, except that an adult rider may carry a child securely attached to his person in a back pack or sling.

625 ILCS 5/11-1504 CLINGING TO VEHICLES No person riding upon any bicycle, coaster, roller skates, sled or toy vehicle shall attach the same or himself to any vehicle upon a roadway.

625 ILCS 5/11-1505 RIDING BICYCLES UPON ROADWAY Persons riding bicycles upon a roadway shall not ride more than 2 abreast, except on paths or parts of the roadway set aside for their exclusive use. Persons riding 2 abreast shall not impede the normal and reasonable movement of traffic and, on a laned roadway, shall ride within a single lane subject to the provisions of Section 11-1505 (625 ILCS 5/11-1505).

625 ILCS 5/11-1506 CARRYING ARTICLES No person operating a bicycle shall carry any package, bundle or article which prevents the use of both hands in the control and operation of the bicycle. A person operating a bicycle shall keep at least one hand on the handlebars at all times.

625 ILCS 5/11-1507 LAMPS AND OTHER EQUIPMENT ON BICYCLES

    (a) Every bicycle, when in use at night time, shall be equipped with a lamp on the front, which shall emit white light visible from a distance of at least 500 feet to the front and with a red reflector on the rear, of a type approved by the Department, which shall be visible from all distances from 100 feet to 600 feet to the rear when directly in front of lawful lower beams of headlamps on a motor vehicle. A lamp emitting a red light visible from a distance of 500 feet to the rear may be used in addition to the red reflector.

    (b) A bicycle shall not be equipped with nor shall any person use upon a bicycle any siren.

    (c) Every bicycle shall be equipped with a brake which will adequately control movement of an stop and hold such bicycle.

625 ILCS 5/11-1509 A uniformed police officer may at any time upon reasonable cause to believe that a bicycle is unsafe or not equipped as required by law, or that its equipment is not in proper adjustment or repair, require the person riding the bicycle to stop and submit the bicycle to an inspection and such text with reference thereto as may be appropriate.

American Bike Trails publishes and distributes
maps, books and guides for the bicyclist.

For more information:
www.abtrails.com